# WORKING
## ◄ ON ►
## SEVERN & CANAL

### REMINISCENCES *of*
### WORKING BOATMEN

*Hugh Conway-Jones*

By the Same Author

*Gloucester Docks – An Illustrated History*
*A Guide to Gloucester Docks*

# WORKING LIFE ‹ON› SEVERN & CANAL

## REMINISCENCES *of* WORKING BOATMEN

Compiled by
Hugh Conway-Jones

ALAN SUTTON

First published in the United Kingdom in 1990 by
Alan Sutton Publishing Limited · Brunswick Road · Gloucester

First published in the United States of America in 1990 by
Alan Sutton Publishing Inc. · Wolfeboro Falls · NH 03896–0848

British Library Cataloguing in Publication Data
Conway-Jones, Hugh
Working life on Severn and canal.
1. England. Inland waterway freight transport services:
Severn & Canal carrying company, history
I. Title
386.2440942

ISBN 0–86299–745–3

Library of Congress Cataloging in Publication Data applied for

*Cover photograph: Severn and Canal Carrying Company boats at Gas Street Basin in Birmingham*

Typeset in 10/12pt Palatino
Typesetting and origination by
Alan Sutton Publishing Limited
Printed in Great Britain
Dotesios Printers Limited

# Contents

# Sources for Illustrations

Harry Arnold/Waterway Images Collection 92; Birmingham Reference Library 45, 60, 62; Black Country Museum 88; Boat Museum, Ellesmere Port 47, 162; British Waterways Archives 137, 167 (upper); Cadbury's Ltd. 64, 73, 74, 79, 90; R. Dudfield 83; Stanley Gardiner Collection 86; Gloucester Museum 94; Charles Hinman Collection 33, 55, 103, 108, 111, 118, 134, 145, 149, 152, 175; Stanley Holland Collection 16, 37, 43, 68, 76, 99, 142, 155; Kidderminster Library 71; David McDougall Collection 6, 36, 42, 50; National Waterways Museum, Gloucester 8, 127; National Waterways Museum, Gloucester, Harry Roberts Collection 17, 22, 98, 101, 105, 115, 117, 123, 132, 147, 159, 167, 171; cover; Port of Bristol Authority 177; Royal Commission on the Historic Monuments of England 3, 25, 29, 31; Brian Standish 51; Alf Thomas Collection 10, 20, 113, 129, 138, 140, 151, 160, 168; Walwins Photographic 12; Peter White Collection 9, 172; Ian Wright Collection 58.

# Preface

This book was inspired by the late Alfie Thomas, who worked on the Severn for most of his life and believed that the story of the boatmen should be told. To get other viewpoints, I also talked to James Dudfield, Charlie Mayo, Tom Mayo, Terry Payton, Reg Price, Harry Roberts, Frank Savage, Bill Stokes, Arthur Thompson and Albert Tonks. I spent many enjoyable evenings hearing of the working practices and hardships of life afloat between the two world wars, and I learned to respect the skills that had been handed down from one generation to another. I have concentrated mainly on the carrying of dry cargoes which has such a long history on the Severn, and have only touched briefly on the enormous traffic in petroleum products which is really another story.

I tape recorded most of these conversations, and it is the transcriptions of these tapes that form the basis of this book. As many topics were mentioned in more than one conversation, I have mixed contributions from different sources and edited them to provide a readable account, with each chapter covering a different aspect of the whole. Inevitably, this has meant using a certain amount of editorial licence to change grammar and insert additional words of explanation to help the story flow, and some of these insertions are highlighted by the use of italics. I am conscious that memories are imperfect and my interpretation of some details may be faulty, but I hope I have given a fair impression of the life of these boatmen that would otherwise go unrecorded.

To supplement the memories, I have used written sources to provide an introductory chapter on the historical development of carrying on the Severn and a later chapter on the transformation of the Severn and Canal Carrying Company for which most of the boatmen worked. I am also grateful for information received from David McDougall, Philip Morgan, R.T. Pilkington and Fred Rowbotham.

Finally, I would like to acknowledge the support of my family that has given me the freedom to present this account of a style of life that has now gone forever.

Hugh Conway-Jones

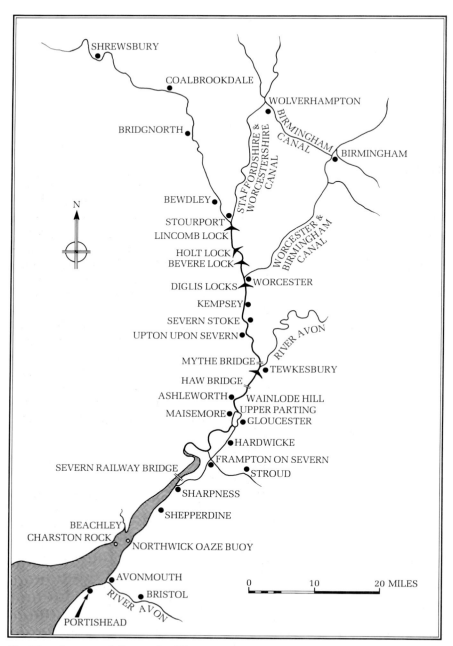

The River Severn and Connecting Waterways

# Severn Carriers

The River Severn has long been an important route for transporting goods between the Midlands and the great port of Bristol, and it played a vital part in the development of the metal-using industries of Birmingham and the Black Country. By the seventeenth century, there was a well established system of carrying on the river, with vessels regularly trading between Bristol and the riverside towns as far up as Shrewsbury. Vessels carried agricultural and industrial products down river, and in return brought back raw materials and imported luxury goods. There was also a growing traffic in coal from the Shropshire pits to towns as far south as Gloucester.

The vessels using the upper reaches did not usually carry much cargo because of the shallows in the natural river. Above Worcester, in particular, there were numerous outcrops of hard rocks and gravel shoals which meant that at times of low water, the river was little better than a series of pools separated every mile or so by rock-bars over which the depth of water might not exceed 18 in. The lower river between Worcester and Gloucester had similar shallows, but high spring tides ran to Upton upon Severn, and by hindering the down-flowing fresh water, caused a rise of 18 in at Worcester.

In the eighteenth century, the barges and frigates using the upper river were 40 to 60 ft in length with a single mast and a square sail. They were capable of carrying 20 to 40 tons, depending on the depth of water available, and most were used in the coal trade, although some carried general cargoes which were trans-shipped to and from larger vessels at down-river wharfs. These larger vessels were known as trows (pronounced to rhyme with crows). They were about 60 ft long with main and top masts having two square sails, and some also had a mizzen mast with a lateen sail. These could carry 80 to 100 tons and were capable of going down the estuary to Bristol and sometimes further afield. In a survey carried out in 1756, as many as 367 vessels were noted on the river, of which most would have been classed as barges or frigates as 304 of them were owned at places from Bewdley upwards.

1

Where possible, these vessels used their sails up the river, taking advantage of the tides between Gloucester and Tewkesbury, but often they had to be towed by gangs of six or eight men hauling on a line from the mast-head. An Act of 1532 had confirmed the right of the king's subjects to use a path 1½ ft wide on each side of the river for hauling boats, although in practice the men just had to struggle along the natural river bank as best they could, sometimes bending themselves to the ground in their endeavours to make progress against the current.

During the eighteenth century, the longer distance traffic going down to Bristol and South Wales included agricultural products and manufactured goods from Cheshire and the north brought by pack-horse to Bewdley, iron products and earthenware from the Black Country, salt from Droitwich and corn from Tewkesbury and the Vale of Evesham. Up-river cargoes included luxury foodstuffs and consumables imported through Bristol, raw materials needed by the industries of the Midlands and the north-west, and agricultural products and manufactured goods from the west of England. There was a considerable growth in this traffic during the eighteenth century, and it seems that this was accompanied by a move towards larger vessels working in the estuary with more trans-shipment from the smaller vessels that were still needed on the upper river.

One contribution to the growth in traffic was the opening in 1772 of the Staffordshire and Worcestershire Canal which joined the Severn at Stourport. This had a junction with the Birmingham Canal and later with the Trent and Mersey and the Stourbridge Canals, with Stourport becoming an important trans-shipment point for ironware, glass, pottery and textiles going to Bristol for export. These developments highlighted the poor state of the river, with traffic being impeded by shallows in the summer and by floods in the winter. Water levels had always been variable, but the fluctuations were made worse by improvements in drainage which allowed rain-water to run off the fields much faster. Towards the end of the eighteenth century, navigation above Worcester was stopped for an average of nearly two months every year, and the bad shoals at Upton upon Severn and Wainlode held up boats on occasions for as long as three or four weeks. In the winter, there was usually sufficient depth of water, but then the low bridge at Upton could be troublesome.

In spite of these difficulties, there was considerable traffic on the river when conditions allowed. Firms of Severn carriers operated reasonably regular services between the up-river towns and Bristol. In 1790 there were ten vessels trading from Bewdley and above, seven from Stour-port, four from Worcester, six from Tewkesbury/Upton and five from Gloucester. These voyages were not without their dangers, and the pages of the *Gloucester Journal* reported many mishaps. In 1791, the trow *Thomas* was returning to Upton upon Severn deeply laden with oilcake when she was hit by a coal barge not far north of Gloucester and sank with the loss of all her cargo. In another incident the trow *John* of Bewdley, laden with iron, kelp and deal balks, was sailing up the river above Gloucester when a sudden shift of wind caused her to capsize and one man was drowned. Later a Shrewsbury barge was also capsized by a sudden gust of wind near Kempsey, and a passenger trapped in the cabin of the vessel was drowned.

To try to improve the navigation, the Staffordshire and Wor-cestershire Canal Company attempted to remove some of the shoals in the 1790s by building timber and stone jetties which would constrict the stream, but the bargemen found the jetties caused a great incon-venience, and Worcester assizes ordered their removal. A more success-ful improvement was the construction of a towing-path, which was

The ketch *Tilly* moored below the nineteenth-century Westgate Bridge at Gloucester. The low arch caused difficulties for the boatmen when the river level was high

completed down to Gloucester in the early 1800s. This allowed horses to be used for towing the vessels in place of men, although the transition was not easy. When horses first appeared at Upton upon Severn, a mob of hauliers tried to prevent them pulling, and a great deal of violence was used which almost amounted to a riot. Another improvement was the removal of the multi-arched Westgate Bridge at Gloucester and its replacement in 1816 by a single-span structure.

A further boost to traffic on the river was the opening of the Worcester and Birmingham Canal in 1815. This provided a more direct route from Birmingham to the south-west, and Worcester became a trans-shipment centre like Stourport. In those days, canal longboats (or narrow boats as they are known in other parts of the country), did not go out on to the river as it was thought they would be swamped and their crews drowned. Therefore, when a boat laden with coal did venture down to Gloucester, many people gathered to witness its arrival. The voyage was considered so hazardous that it was likened to the voyage of Columbus to America, and although this was soon followed by other coal boats, most cargoes to and from Bristol continued to be trans-shipped at Worcester or Stourport.

As well as the difficulties caused by the shallows in the river above Gloucester, the narrow winding stretch to the south had also been a source of delays. It could only be navigated for a few days each month on the spring tides, and groups of vessels would gather at Gloucester and King Road (near the mouth of the Bristol Avon) waiting for the right conditions. This restriction was by-passed by the opening of the Gloucester and Berkeley Canal in 1827, although in practice most local vessels continued to use the river route when they could to avoid having to pay tolls. The opening of the canal also allowed sea-going vessels to go right up to Gloucester, and this resulted in more longboats using the river, picking up cargoes overside from the ships at Gloucester and delivering direct to a customer in the Midlands.

Horse-towing up the river was a big improvement on the earlier use of men, but it was still a slow process hauling against the current. In an effort to speed things up, Humphrey Brown and Son of Tewkesbury introduced the steam tug *Sabrina* in 1830 to tow their own vessels between Gloucester and Worcester. The tug had 14 hp engines, mounted horizontally, possibly to help get under the bridges when the river level was high, and she was able to save forty-eight hours on the time previously taken with horses. Two years later, the tug was involved in an accident near Tewkesbury when she collided with a Worcester trow, which was so badly damaged that she sank. It is not clear if the tug continued operating after this incident.

By the 1830s, there was a marked reduction in the number of regular carriers trading between Bristol and places above Stourport. This was partly due to the increased use of trans-shipment at intermediate places and also because an alternative access was provided to the area when the Shrewsbury Canal was linked to the main system in 1835. In 1840, James Walker reported that the traffic above Gloucester included 3,328 laden canal boats and 84 empties, 405 partly-laden barges, 296 laden trows and 253 partly laden. Craft from Shropshire were often held up by shallows at Ironbridge, and when the water rose, they came down to Gloucester in fleets of twenty or thirty and tried to unload as quickly as possible so they could get back again before the water level fell.

In the interim, a railway between Birmingham and Gloucester had been proposed which would avoid Worcester, and this at last prompted serious consideration of ways of improving the river. Initially, a private company was formed to construct locks and carry out dredging, but it could not get parliamentary approval. Instead a public body, the Severn Commission, was set up to carry out the work, and financial backing was provided by the Staffordshire and Worcestershire Canal Company. Locks were constructed at Lincomb, Holt, Bevere and Diglis between 1842 and 1844, and dredging was carried out to improve the navigation below Worcester. However, it was soon found that dredging could not maintain the promised 6-ft depth of water, and blasting channels through the natural rock-bars actually made conditions worse because it allowed the water to run away more freely. A plan to build another lock below Worcester was blocked by the Admiralty at first, and it was several years before any further improvements were made. Meanwhile the Severn carriers had to manage as best they could, and the effect of competition from the railways meant that some of the firms were forced to give up and others merged.

Around the middle of the century, there was a major change in the appearance of the trows as most of the old square sails were replaced by fore-and-aft rigs. The larger trows usually became gaff-rigged ketches, and the smaller trows just had a mainsail with one or two foresails. The traditional trow had an open hold with side cloths to keep out the spray, but some were later decked and had hatch coamings to make them more sea-worthy. They had a flat bottom to facilitate working in shallow waters, and they carried a detachable keel that could be fixed in place by chains when sailing in the estuary.

Iron trows moored near the Tontine Hotel at Stourport

The next change to the navigation of the river came in 1853, when the old bridge at Upton upon Severn was replaced with a girder bridge which had one section that could be moved to let vessels pass through. Another development that year was the re-introduction of steam tugs for towing on the river. The Severn Steam Tug Company, backed by the Staffordshire and Worcestershire Canal Company, brought the paddle tug *Enterprise* round from London, and this was so successful that two larger paddle tugs *Reliance* and *Resolution* were put into service in 1855. When the state of the river was favourable, they could tow several barges and canal boats from Gloucester to Stourport in 15 to 18 hr, less than half the time it took with horses, although during dry periods there were still difficulties due to shoals below Worcester.

After much discussion and lobbying, the Severn Commission eventually obtained approval to build another lock at Upper Lode near Tewkesbury, and this was opened in 1858. It was made much larger than the locks higher up the river in order to accommodate a tug and all its tow in one locking. Two years later, the Staffordshire and Worcestershire Canal Company backed the introduction of two cargo steamers *Edmund Ironsides* and *Cuirassier*. It was intended that they would help to develop the china clay traffic to the Potteries, but the condition of the river below Tewkesbury made the trade unreliable. After further deliberations, the Severn Commission built weirs and locks at Llanthony below Gloucester and at Maisemore in 1871, and these at last ensured a reliable depth of water for the whole route from Gloucester to Stourport.

By this time, there were only two firms acting as long distance Severn carriers for general cargoes – Danks & Sanders and Fellows & Co. These two merged in 1874 to form the Severn and Canal Carrying Shipping and Steam Towing Company (later shortened to Severn and Canal Carrying Company). This new firm had a dozen trows, half-a-dozen lighters, about fifty canal longboats and four tugs. The tugs operated a regular service on the river and, although giving preference to the company's own vessels, they also provided a service for the many other small traders who carried specific cargoes such as coal and hay above Gloucester. A large new dock at Sharpness was also opened in 1874, and the Gloucester and Berkeley Canal Company bought the Worcester and Birmingham Canal, becoming the Sharpness New Docks and Gloucester and Birmingham Navigation Company (or Dock Company for short).

During the 1880s, there was pressure on the Severn Commission to make further improvements that would allow larger vessels to use the river, and a programme of lock deepening and dredging was carried out during the early 1890s. When the work was complete, Severn and Canal arranged a trip to Worcester for their steamer *Atalanta* (74 tons reg.), which had been built at Bristol in 1884 by G.K. Stothert & Co., but the trial was not successful and no real increase in traffic resulted from the improvements.

During the early years of the twentieth century, the Severn and Canal Carrying Company fought a desperate battle for survival against competition from the railways. To provide a full service to customers, they had to maintain a large fleet that could respond quickly when a ship arrived at one of the Bristol Channel ports. They also needed warehouse and delivery facilities in the Midlands, but the rates they could charge barely covered the costs, and they needed the profits from towing other vessels on the river. Matters were particularly bad in 1903, and in the following year the company was reformed as a subsidiary of Fellows Morton and Clayton who operated canal boats between London, the Midlands and Manchester. The new company quickly approached the Dock Company to seek a rebate on tolls, and after lengthy negotiations, the Dock Company agreed to a 50 per cent discount on through traffic passing between the lower estuary ports and the Midlands.

SS *Atalanta* at Worcester 1895

This agreement enabled Severn and Canal to go ahead with the purchase of new barges and tugs, and a good deal of fresh traffic was obtained. However, the Dock Company directors were concerned about the high rates being charged for towing on the river, and prompted by other boat owners, they decided to start running their own tugs charging lower rates from April 1906. Severn and Canal pleaded that they couldn't carry on without the profits from the towing, and after discussions with the Dock Company failed to reach any compromise, they announced they were giving up.

This resulted in the formation of a third Severn and Canal Carrying Company which was largely financed by local grain and timber merchants, with some shares held by the Dock Company. The new company sold their five tugs to the Dock Company at valuation, and they were allowed to lease warehouses at Gloucester, Worcester and Birmingham for a peppercorn rent. They were able to win back some traffic from the railways, but the freight rates obtainable were so low that the company was still losing money and needed further assistance. The Dock Company realized that they ought to help, not only because Severn and Canal traffic was a direct source of income, but also because their operations helped to keep the railway rates down and so benefited

Longboats belonging to Severn and Canal and other owners at Sharpness

the wider trade of the port. After lengthy negotiations, therefore, the Dock Company eventually agreed in 1908 to hand over the profits from the river towing in exchange for the right to nominate a majority of the directors, thus maintaining control of what towing rates were actually charged.

The centre of operations became firmly established at Gloucester, where the company leased two warehouses beside the Old Arm [Barge Arm], and incoming cargoes were trans-shipped from trows to longboats. The company also had warehouses at Bristol, Worcester, Stourport and Birmingham, as well as a dock-yard and workshops at Stourport where their vessels were overhauled. The sails were taken off

Severn and Canal Carrying Company warehouses and boats at Gloucester

the trows which became dumb barges towed by tugs, although masts and spars were retained for cargo handling. The main dumb barges were *Nelson* and *Togo* (80 tons reg.), built at Beverley in 1905, and there were also a number of iron trows (40–70 tons reg.) built at Bristol and Cardiff between 1858 and 1876. Two motor barges, *Osric* and *Serlo* (40 tons reg.), were built at Dartmouth in 1913 by Simpson Strickland & Co., and the steamer *Atalanta* was given a two-cylinder Bolinder engine in 1916. The company also had a large fleet of longboats based at Gloucester, which were towed up the river by tugs, and then horses were picked up at Worcester to take the boats on to their destinations.

*It is the reminiscences of the men who worked on these barges, tugs and longboats that form the basis of this book, and the stories which follow are largely told in their own words.*

# CHAPTER 1

# *Barge Traffic to Gloucester*

*In the 1920s, the Severn and Canal Carrying Company had a fleet of barges that met ships discharging in ports around the Bristol Channel and brought their cargoes up to Gloucester for trans-shipment into longboats. Three of the barges had their own engines, and the others were towed by the motor barges or by tugs.*

On each dumb barge you had a skipper and two mates. It was better pay than on the longboats that went up to the Midlands, so young men from the boats transferred to the barges when they could prove they were strong enough to carry sacks of wheat which weighed $2\frac{1}{4}$ cwt. To learn how to do it, you watched how the older boatmen carried the sacks over their shoulders and dropped them down in the hold of their boat, and you asked if you could help. I carried about twenty sacks the first time so as not to overdo it, as it made my shoulders and back bleed. It was surprising how quickly the skin healed up, but when I took on another lot, it was torture as all the scabs were fetched off and it started bleeding again. I had to go on though – you could only learn the hard way. There was an art in carrying the sacks and there was an art in dropping them down so you didn't have to move them. If you chucked them down any way, you had to pull them into place, and that took longer and used up your strength. When I thought I had enough experience, I told the foreman. He arranged to bring a boat alongside a barge to be discharged, and I had to carry 300 sacks to load the boat in an hour and a half. Once I demonstrated I could carry the sacks in this way, they offered me a job on the barges as soon as one came available.

Most of the trips were concerned with collecting imports from Avonmouth and Bristol, but some barges also went to Newport, Cardiff,

11

Swansea and Bridgwater. In the 1920s, a lot of wheat was carried on its way to mills in the Midlands, but this traffic reduced as the milling industry concentrated at the ports. Large quantities of metals were also carried, together with a wide variety of foodstuffs and general cargoes brought on the Bristol City ships from America and the Holland Steamship Company steamers from the Continent. There were few outgoing cargoes, and most of the barges left Gloucester empty, but some manufactured goods from the Midlands were taken for export.

For the crew of a dumb barge, the orders were usually to go to Avonmouth or Bristol and bring back a cargo for Gloucester. If a Severn and Canal motor barge was also going to the same port, they took you all the way. Otherwise you started off with one of the regular Dock Company tugs such as *Moss Rose, Mayflower, Violet, Myrtle, Hazel* or *Speedwell*. One of these usually left from the Western Wall just below Llanthony Bridge at 8 o'clock every morning and another at 1 o'clock.

Also in the tow might be empty trows, timber lighters and longboats. The tug skipper put any trows first because they were able to steer better, then lighters came next and the longboats were on the back of the lighters, breasted up. An average tow was three or four trows and lighters with perhaps two or three longboats. The longboats were

The Dock Company's steam tug *Mayflower* towing empty barges down the canal

usually going to Cadbury's factory at Frampton, about half way down the canal, but if there was a special cargo to collect at Sharpness, there could be a dozen or more longboats in the tow. It is difficult to steer empty boats, so they were all kept on short ropes, close up together, but even so if there was any wind across the canal, you could still have a bit of a job keeping up to windward and getting through the bridges. The empty boats tended to go in snake fashion, and so they always tried to put a loaded boat on the back to hold the others straight. If there was no loaded boat, the last one in the line could tow a bucket behind, but if the tug skipper ever found out, he'd go mad as it was like pulling an extra boat.

The bridges down the canal swung open in two halves, and so they needed a man each side to work them. There was a bridgeman to open one side, but in the early days, one of the crew of the last boat had to open the other side. Approaching a bridge, the last boats put their helms over so that the stern of one almost touched the bank, and a man jumped off and ran ahead to open the bridge. When the whole tow had passed through, he closed the bridge, ran along the tow-path, and the boats swung into the bank again to pick him up. The men didn't like all the running they had to do, and after the union took up the matter, the Dock Company employed passmen who cycled along the tow-path and worked all the bridges. One started with the tug from Gloucester and another with the tug from Sharpness, and wherever they met, they turned round and came back home with the other tow. One of the passmen used to stop for a drink at the Pilot Inn [at Hardwicke], and one time he was still in there when the tug arrived. The tug sounded its whistle to get him out, but he wouldn't be hurried! How he managed to ride his bike along the tow-path after that, I'll never know, but I don't think he ever fell in the canal.

The tug skipper blew two whistles if he wanted both sides of a bridge open for a normal tow, but if he was going solo, he could get through one side and so he'd only blow one. Approaching Sharpness, he had to blow three to get the Severn Railway Bridge open, two for the High Level Bridge and one if he only wanted the Low Level Bridge. He only needed the higher bridges open if there was a trow in the tow with a high mast.

Once in the dock at Sharpness, the tug gave you a start and then cast off so you drifted down to the bottom of the dock, and you moored there until it was time to go through the lock into the tidal basin well before high water. The usual channel tugs were *Resolute* and *Primrose*, and they could take as many as five or six barges. One of them worked on every tide, night and day, unless it was too rough or too foggy. Leaving the tidal basin, the tug skipper had to take notice of the signals on the watch house. If there were two balls up, one each side of the yard arm, that meant the entrance was shut. If there was one ball up, you could go out, and if there was no ball up, vessels could come in. When the tide was finished, they put the two balls up again, and the lock-keepers could go home.

If you left before high water, the tide would still be running up to Gloucester, and as you rounded the pier, the tug had to turn dead into the current. Then you could stand still for some time with full throttle before you started to make headway as the tide eased. Going down to Avonmouth, the tug skippers had to be very experienced as that part of the Bristol Channel has strong currents and many rocks. It seemed as though you always went on a night tide, and you couldn't sleep very well because it was a most dangerous place to be – especially in any wind.

The course you could steer depended on how big was the tide. If the tide didn't come up to 18 ft at Sharpness, you had to follow the channel, but if it was a big tide, you'd go round the pier and then creep down close to the shore. In this way, you'd get the first of the ebb to help you while the last of the flood was still going up the middle. While one tug was creeping down the shore like this, the deck-hand was concerned to see a woman in the water. He reported this to the skipper, who asked if she was standing or swimming. On being told she was swimming, the skipper said 'Good – that means there's enough water for us to keep going.'

The channel is marked by a series of leading lights, buoys and beacons. The leading lights are in pairs and the tug skipper kept the two in one until he picked up the alignment of the next pair. Before the war, they were all oil lamps, and sometimes they were blown out so he had a job to find his way. At Shepperdine, the channel crosses over to Slime Road on the Welsh side. You kept outside Lyde Rock and Chapel Rock off Beachley, went on towards Charston Rock off Portskewett and then crossed back to the English side past the two beacons marking the Shoots. The tide was always running across your course when you got down there, so you had to steer into the tide a bit to counteract its effect. When you got through the Shoots, the tug steered south-south-west and that took you to Avonmouth.

One night *Primrose* got to Charston with four barges, when bang –

they went into fog so thick the skipper couldn't see the bow of the tug! It was a worrying time, but that's what he had a compass for. He knew he had to steer south for about twelve minutes, and then he altered course to south-south-west. After steaming for a further thirty minutes without seeing anything, one of the bargemen behind got worried and shouted that they were going the wrong side of Avonmouth pier. But the mate on the tug told him to shut up as the skipper knew where he were going, and just then they heard the gong on the end of the pier and all was well.

By the time you got to Avonmouth, the tide was more than half-ebbed out and the dock gates were closed. So the tug took you round into the Old Entrance (what we called the Old Way), and you tied up there alongside the pier. As the tide ebbed, the barges lay on the bottom and then you could get your head down for a nice sleep while the tug went off to Portishead to anchor in the pill there.

When it was time for the gates to open, the lock men blew their whistle, and you worked the barge through the lock by running a line ashore and using a capstan by the lock or the winch on the foredeck of the barge. Every vessel entering Avonmouth had to be recorded, and one time when a new harbour-master was on duty, he shouted to a skipper 'What's the name of your barge?' When the skipper replied 'Wye', the harbour-master thought his authority was being questioned, and he began to get annoyed. The matter was only resolved when the skipper took him to the bow to see the name written there!

Once into the dock at Avonmouth, there was a small tug run by Perrys that took you to where you had to go. In the early days, we often loaded wheat or maize from a floating pneumatic elevator which could suck the grain out of a ship's hold and store it. We went alongside the elevator, and they lowered down a stage on chains inside the barge. There were two pipes for the grain to come down, and a machine released two hundredweight and a quarter at a time to fill a sack. A man stood by each pipe, and when his sack was full, he tied it up and tipped it down on to the stage. You took the sacks from one man and stowed them at one end of the barge while your mate was doing the same at the other end. When you had each end quarter loaded, you both reversed and filled up the two middle quarters. The skipper stood by in case any of the sacks fell badly, and he put them right so you could take them from the stage. You carried the sacks on your shoulders, and even for that short distance, it half killed you – it was murder at times. The sacks kept coming, and if you were not back in time for the next, the skipper soon let you know – he'd call you everything! There was many a time that my back was bleeding, but it got hardened up after a few months.

There were many other cargoes to collect from Avonmouth, particularly metals like copper and spelter [zinc], and you usually received them directly over the side of the ship. Some copper came in long thin ingots that we called cigars, and they were lifted out of the ship in bundles with a chain round each end. The best of these were very clean and specially marked with some kind of chalk you couldn't rub out, and they reckoned these went to the mint in Birmingham. There were also some flat blocks of copper about 18 in square and 2 in thick that we called cathodes. They had very rough edges and you had to be careful lifting them or else they cut your hands to pieces. Also cocoa beans for Cadbury's came from the Gold Coast [Ghana] where Cadbury's had their own plantations. In the 1920s, there were only occasional shipments of 200 to 300 tons, but this traffic developed later.

If you were going to Bristol rather than Avonmouth, you waited in the Old Entrance for the B stol tug to pick you up on the next tide. He took you up the Avon to the Cumberland Basin, and then you locked up into what we called the Float [the Floating Harbour]. A small tug took you over to Bush's Corner by Princestreet Bridge, and you moored there

The iron trow *Severn* partly loaded with boxes of Typhoo tea

*Atalanta* loading from the Dutch steamer *Zaanstroom* at Bristol

alongside the wharf. The Bristol City steamers from America and the Holland Steamship Company steamers from the Continent moored just opposite, and when they wanted you by a ship, you had to get the barge alongside. We had a winch with a tremendous long line, and we carried our own boat. So you skulled the boat across carrying the line, made it fast on the ship, and then went back and winched the barge across alongside the ship. It was hard work, but it was the only way you could get about. Then the ship unloaded over the side using its own gear.

We had to collect all kinds of things, from big rolls of polished sheet steel for the car industry in Birmingham to barrels of American gum. Also we had 5 gal drums of carbide which were placed in one part of the barge separated with sheets over in case you had a bad passage and water got down on top of them. The Holland steamers brought 50- or 100-ton lots of strawboard that Cadbury's used for making boxes and cartons. They also brought tremendous big rolls of paper, about 5 tons in a roll, and we put about sixteen rolls in a barge. We had lots of cases of foodstuff like Libby's milk, Carnation milk and corned beef. Many a case was damaged in handling, and you stowed it where you could reach it easily later. Then you went into the hold at night and removed a few tins. Nobody noticed. When you got to Gloucester, you marked the case with a blue chalk and told the foreman. He put a note on the order to tell Birmingham that it came out of the ship damaged.

It was not until a ship arrived that the Severn and Canal office at Bristol got to know what was on board. Then they telephoned to Gloucester to get some barges down as soon as possible. But the dockers had to start unloading the ship, and so the carters might have to be brought in to take some of the stuff by horse and cart round to our warehouse, a big wooden shed on the Grove not far from Princestreet Bridge. Also, if there was some cargo left in the ship at the end and they didn't have any of our barges to put it in, it was taken to our warehouse and we picked up from there later. There was no crane at our warehouse, so we used the mast and boom on the barge and set up a block and tackle worked by the winch. *Osric, Serlo* and *Atalanta* had motors that could work the lifting gear, but on the trows you had to use the hand winch. Sometimes we had to load rolls of paper weighing about 5 tons, but the skippers were very experienced. They knew just how to rig up pulleys and ropes so that when you picked up 5 tons, it seemed like it was only 5 cwt. As you worked the winch, the skipper guided the rope so it ran level on the barrel. If it tangled up and then slipped off with a 5-ton load on the boom, it could fetch the whole lot down.

When you finished loading, you went on the Bristol tug down the Avon and back into the Old Entrance at Avonmouth. On the next tide, the Sharpness tug took you round into the New Entrance, picked up the barges from Avonmouth and brought you all back.

Coming up with the tide, the worst part was from the Shoots to where the channel widens again past Beachley. Off Beachley, there are some underwater rocks known as the Benches, and on a big tide these can make the water boil up like mushrooms. The swirl of the water could move a barge up towards the tug, leaving a slack rope, and if the barge then ran back, the rope could fly up and break leaving you in all sorts of trouble. Also turning round the Lyde Rock into the slack water of Slime Road, there was a big swirl there that could swing the barge round, so the tug skipper had to be prepared to cut his engine right down until the rope came up steady, and then he could wind her up again.

To add to the hazards, there were lots of times you suddenly ran into fog. *Primrose* went ashore in fog near the Chapel Rock once, and as a barge she was towing was carried past on the tide, the rope broke and the barge went off up the river with two men on board. It was early flood tide and the tug soon floated off again, but it was still thick and the skipper had no idea where the barge had gone. All he could do was to drop the anchor with the one barge he had left. He waited there a few hours, and as the tide was falling again, he suddenly saw the missing barge come right back alongside. Much to the relief of the men on board, he was able to take it in tow and go back to Avonmouth.

There were very few places where you could anchor in the estuary, and if you were coming across the Counts Channel from the Welsh side and you ran into dense fog, the tug had to keep going. Even if he couldn't see a thing, the skipper knew what course he had to steer, and as he approached the shore, he'd blow four whistles and a short one, and the light-keeper at Shepperdine rang a bell. That gave the skipper some idea where he was, and he kept creeping in until he went right up on the mud with the barges as well. That was a safe place to wait until the next tide when usually the fog had cleared.

To get a tow into Sharpness, the tug had to swing round before the entrance to head into the tide and then drop back slowly. The skipper had to judge it to get there at just the right time, about twenty minutes to flow. If he was too soon on a big tide, he couldn't hold the barges against the current, and so sometimes he waited for a bit at Slime Road on the way up. On a big tide he'd swing at the Swinging Light well before the entrance, but on a smaller tide, he could swing just before the south pier. As the flood tide eased off, the skipper aimed to be near the end of the pier, and when they dropped the ball down to show there was nothing coming out, he turned the tug into the entrance. The barge skippers had to steer carefully during this turning manoeuvre to ensure the ropes didn't go slack, because if a slack rope suddenly set up and broke, the barge would be carried past the entrance.

Once you'd locked up into the dock, you waited for the regular canal tug to take you up to Gloucester. Passing Cadbury's factory at Frampton, one or two longboats might throw a rope across and join on the back of the tow. The boatmen had to be careful their ropes were properly coiled and ran out freely during this operation. On one occasion, a man lost his foot when it became caught in a coil of rope that pulled tight around a timberhead. Approaching Gloucester, boys would sometimes swim out to the tow and try to hang on to a rope which sagged enough between the boats for a swimmer to catch hold of. They were towed along like that for a bit of fun, and then they swam ashore and ran back along the tow-path. But some of the boatmen didn't approve of this, and they threatened to throw something to make the boys let go. Normally, you cast off from the tug approaching Llanthony Bridge and drifted up into the dock, but if it was a heavy tow, you weren't going fast enough, and the tug had to pull you up into the dock.

At Gloucester, most of the cargoes were transferred directly into longboats using the electric crane on the front of the Severn and Canal warehouse or the two derricks around the corner by the Old Arm [Barge Arm]. For unloading sacks, one member of the barge crew worked in the hold and another stood on the deck. On the end of the hoist rope was a length of chain called a snorter. As this came down, the chap in the hold looped it over the neck of a sack and he whistled to tell the hoist man to start lifting. When the sack was pulled up, the other man caught hold of it and let it slide down his leg on to a stage hanging over the side of the barge from which the longboat men could take it. He loosened the snorter, and threw it back into the barge ready for the next sack. The man in the hold had to be careful because you always had two or three spectators leaning on the barge, and one of them might whistle early. The hoist man was very quick, and there were cases where the hoist started working while the snorter was still round the chaps wrist. Then there was a great shout of 'Wo!' which made the hoist man curse and swear, and he started to chase after whoever had whistled! When you'd finished discharging, you took the barge and tied her up in a berth

*Atalanta* and *Wye* being unloaded at Gloucester

where she'd be all right for a few days, and then you waited your turn for another trip.

Sometimes barges had to go to one of the South Wales ports, and then you didn't usually use the canal and channel tugs. When there was a cargo to collect, one of the Severn and Canal motor vessels, *Osric, Serlo* or *Atalanta*, went direct to these ports, towing a dumb barge when necessary. You went down the channel on the ebb tide past Avonmouth, and you anchored in the roads until the tide turned and the water rose high enough for you to go into port.

On occasions you met some quite rough weather in the Bristol Channel, and it was necessary to change plans to avoid it. On one trip in *Atalanta*, we were anchored in Cardiff Roads when the skipper picked up a forecast on his cat's-whisker radio that there was a gale expected which would bring big waves coming in there. We couldn't wait for the water to get high enough to go into the docks, and so we had to get out of Cardiff Roads and make for Bridgwater where there would be calmer water. We dashed down to the engine room to get the blow lamps on to the engine because it was a hot bulb start and it always took fifteen or twenty minutes to get her going. As soon as the bulbs were hot enough, you turned on the oil, but if you tried to start it a bit too soon it wouldn't work. Eventually we got it going, and we upped the anchor and started heading for Bridgwater.

On the way there, we were going upside down nearly, and I was feeling none too good. They chucked me in the engine room while the proper driver [engineer] was up in the wheelhouse with the skipper and the mate. Down in the engine room, fuel that had leaked into the drip tray was slopping over the edge and dropping on to the hot cylinder heads causing tremendous white smoke with an awful searing smell. I was on my hands and knees because they'd said the lower you got down the better chance you had of breathing. They knew I wasn't feeling very well, but they were shouting down the speaking tube 'Here she goes' and 'Up she comes'. Then they said once more 'Down she goes,' and I said 'And I hope she never comes up!' Oh my gosh! It was like I'd dropped a bomb near them all.

When we got to Bridgwater, the skipper said 'Pack your things and get on the shore. All the time since I've been at sea, never have I heard anybody wish my ship would never come up again. It's an omen of bad luck.' So he got on the telephone to Gloucester and told our boss that he'd put me ashore and he wasn't going to bring me back. He was going to give me the money for the railway ticket and I had to come back to

Gloucester by rail. But the boss told him not to leave me and, after an argument, we all went back to Cardiff again.

Sometimes at Cardiff we loaded Russian wheat from a pneumatic elevator like those at Avonmouth. On other trips, we went to the Roath Dock to pick up Canadian wheat. Here it was stored in bulk in a warehouse, and the dockers bushelled it up into sacks. They put four bushels into each sack and then checked the weight. The man at the scales had a little scoop, and he took some out or added more to get it right. Then they trucked the sacks across to the quayside and tipped them into your barge. You let the first sacks fall down and put them square to make a stage. Then the skipper stood there to receive the other sacks, and he turned each one over on to your shoulders so you could carry it away and stow it.

Returning from Cardiff, you had to go into Avonmouth to wait for the next tide. By the time you got there, it was about high water, so you couldn't go any further towards Sharpness or else you'd be caught by the falling tide. Once I was on *Togo* being towed by *Osric*, and we were trying to make Cardiff to Avonmouth with a load of wheat. Leaving Cardiff, the skipper of *Osric* thought he had about 3 hr of favourable tide, and even if he could only get to Portishead, it would still suit him.

The motor barge *Osric* leaving Gloucester docks towing *Togo* while the Dock Company's tug *Moss Rose* prepares to pick up a tow

But we had to go 'channel about' round the sandbanks, and because of bad weather, by the time we got where we could have gone straight, the tide had turned. So we spent about 3 hr stuck alongside the English and Welsh Grounds lightship with a full gale blowing. We never went ahead and we never went astern, and all the time we heard that lightship singing out a horrible row. Some of the waves came right over the top of the barge, and one tremendous wave dropped on the fore-and-aft beam and broke it. This beam ran along the centre of the boat to support the hatches and the cloths and when it caved in, the canvas cloths formed a basin resting on the bags of wheat. So all the water coming over the deck was going into this basin, and it put us bow down which was a bit awkward.

We were towing the lifeboat on a very long rope to avoid her running up to the stern of the barge, and then a wave went over and sunk her. The rope didn't break, and we didn't know whether to cut it or not. By cutting it free, we might have saved ourselves a couple of hours instead of towing that thing sunk, but our skipper couldn't tell us what to do as he had got jammed in the companion way and was too worried about himself. We couldn't get him out as he weighed 22 stone, and he was so afraid the barge was going to go down and he was going to drown in that position that he froze. Had it been my decision, I'd have chopped the rope and let the boat go, but we daren't do anything he didn't tell us to do – you couldn't in those days.

When the tide slackened, we made our way to Avonmouth with the captain still stuck in the companion way and the lifeboat dragging behind. Eventually we came alongside the pier, and then he wriggled himself out. He'd had a poor time because he'd wet his trousers half way, and he was glad to go down into his cabin to get some dry clothes! The next morning, we used the motor winch on *Osric* to haul in the lifeboat and tip it up to drain the water out. They got the fire people to come and pump the water out of the canvas basin where the beam had broken and we came up to Gloucester like that.

# CHAPTER 2

# *Longboats to Worcester*

*The Severn and Canal Carrying Company had a fleet of longboats based in Gloucester which carried all kinds of goods up into the Midlands. Cargoes were trans-shipped at Gloucester from the company's barges that were loaded at Avonmouth, Bristol and the South Wales ports, and the longboats also picked up from Cadbury's factory at Frampton (on the Gloucester and Sharpness Canal) and direct from ships at Sharpness and Gloucester.*

The boats were built of wood, and the size was limited to about 70 ft long by 7 ft beam in order to fit in the narrow locks of the Midland canals. Our boats, known as Severners, had bluff bows and were deeper than most canal boats, so they could carry 30 to 33 tons compared with 23 tons for up-country boats. Most of the hull was occupied by the cargo hold which had a false floor to keep the contents clear of any bilge water. Across the width of the hold were three strong beams to support the sides of the boat, and the sections of the hold between the beams were known as the fore-end, fore-middle or back-of-the-mast, stern-middle and the stern-end. The forward beam also supported the mast, and the others supported vertical stands for a line of planks running the full length of the hold. The planks supported the canvas cloths put over the hold when loaded, and we also used them when walking from one end of the boat to the other. Most of the cloths and planks had to be removed for loading and discharging, but a short length at the fore-end, known as the cratch, could be left in place. This was tied down by cotton strings which were scrubbed white to look smart. Also at the front of the hold were stored six to ten balks of wood, 3 or 4 in square, that could be put under heavy cargoes to let the hoist chains pass easily. This dunnage formed a shelf on which the top cloths were kept when not in use.

The space in front of the hold was decked over to form a rope locker, and protruding from this were two posts known as timberheads, one on either side. These were to take the big tow ropes used when going up the river behind a tug, and each had a horizontal steel pin through it to hold the tow rope in place. There was a bilge pump fixed in the foredeck, and the water just came out on the deck and ran over the side. Each boat also had a portable pump which could be used anywhere in the hold by lifting a section of the false floor. The pump was a long tube with a piston and a side spout to throw the water over the side of the boat.

Behind the hold was the cabin, which was about 10 ft long. It had a double bed across the end that could be folded into a cupboard during the day and a side bed which also served as seating. There was a large cupboard with a door that let down to form a table, and there were other cupboards and drawers where space permitted. For heating and cooking, there was usually a small range, and the coal was kept in a box which also served as a step under the entrance doors.

Behind the cabin was an open cockpit for the steerer, known as the hatches, and right at the stern was a small cupboard where food was kept away from the warmth of the cabin. The curved tiller could be fitted into the helm one way for steering, or it could be turned over and cocked up when not in use. After a spell of dry weather, the tiller could become a bit loose in the helm, and then you dipped it in the water for a few

Longboats around the Severn and Canal warehouses at Gloucester

minutes to make it swell up and fit tight again. Each boat had a hook-shaft with a point and a hook at one end for helping to manoeuvre the boat and also a shorter one used to shut the lock gates. On the cabin top was usually a water can secured by a string in case it got knocked off, although some boats had a 5-gal oval barrel or just a stoneware jar. This water was kept for drinking, and water for washing was scooped out of the canal using a hand bowl. For sanitation, it was a matter of 'bucket and chuck it.' Most of the boats were named after places along the routes used, such as *Gloucester, Worcester, Hanbury, Tettenhall, Bilston* and *Walsall*, although some names given by previous owners also remained in use. Each boat had a number as well as a name, and as children we tried to outdo each other in showing off how many we could remember.

You normally only lived on board when you were away on a trip as most crews had their own homes in Gloucester. The skipper was paid for the trip and had to find his own crew, so he usually took one or more members of his own family. It was common for the boatman's wife to act as mate and for young children to go along too, or an older skipper might take a teenager and let the wife stay at home. Children as young as ten would sometimes serve as mate with their father or an uncle, particularly during the school holidays. Also during term time, they'd go away for a week or so and then return to school for a few days before the next trip. If they were away too often, there was pressure from the school authorities, but some missed so much that they left school not being able to read or write. Not surprisingly, many sons followed their fathers on to the boats, and some family names were very well known, such as Manley, Mayo, Spiers, Stokes and Tonks.

It was particularly difficult if the skipper had a large family. Each boat had to be registered with the local health authority, and most were limited to carrying three adults or two adults and two children. There was an inspector to check on this, but if a skipper wanted to take more, he got them on board early in the morning and hid them under the cloths. He'd say to the children 'Now don't forget, if any of you makes a noise, the inspector will come under there and bring you all out.' So they kept as quiet as mice until they were on the way up the river, and then if the inspector wasn't following on his bike, you'd see the heads moving under the canvas and out they came like little rabbits! So sometimes there could be five or six people living in one little box-like cabin, but you couldn't expect to find a healthier group of kids.

In the early days, there were sometimes young boys without homes hanging around who went with any skipper who needed a crew. They had to learn to do what they were told and keep the boat clean, and then they were never long without a trip. If a boatman's wife had to stay at home for a bit, one of the boys would go in her place. Also there were some unmarried skippers who didn't have a regular crew. A few were a bit barbaric and knocked the boys about or half starved them, but others were more considerate. One boy managed to work with two skippers for quite a long time – when he came back with one, if he was lucky, the other would be loaded and tied up by the lock ready to set off next morning. Now and again, the one at Gloucester found his turn came up before the boy was back. So then he sent a postcard to the Worcester office saying he was coming up on the tug, and the boy stayed with the lock-keeper at Worcester until he arrived.

Between trips, the waiting boats were usually moored in the Old Arm [Barge Arm] off the Main Basin at Gloucester where the Company had two large warehouses and its head office. There were about sixty Severn and Canal longboats, and the skippers all had to take their turns based on when they came back from their previous trip. The orders were given out down the bottom of the Old Arm where the crane was and the foreman, Ernie Poole, let the skippers have some choice. He might say 'Who's first? I want two for Walsall and another for Kidderminster.' The first skipper on turn picked what he wanted and then the others followed. You were paid so much a ton for a trip one way, based on the distance involved, and you got some driving money for coming back empty if you didn't get a return load. So one might pick Walsall because it paid more, whereas another would pick Kidderminster which isn't so far and he'd get back quicker. Or the foreman might say 'I want three boats – one to Sharpness, one to Frampton and one to load sugar here for Frampton. What are you going to do?' The first man would choose to load the sugar because, being loaded, he got more money and when he emptied at Frampton he stood a good chance of loading chocolate crumb for Bournville. The second man would choose to go to Frampton because although he'd be empty for that journey, he'd be loading straight away at Frampton. It's hard luck for the third one – he'd have to go empty for much further and might not load in the next two days.

Orders for the 1 o'clock tug down the canal were given out at twelve. That just gave you time to dash home, get a bit of food and then use a hook-shaft to push your boat down below Llanthony Bridge to catch the tug. If there was nothing for you at 1 o'clock, you'd come back at 4 or 5 o'clock for the orders for the following day. If they knew there was a

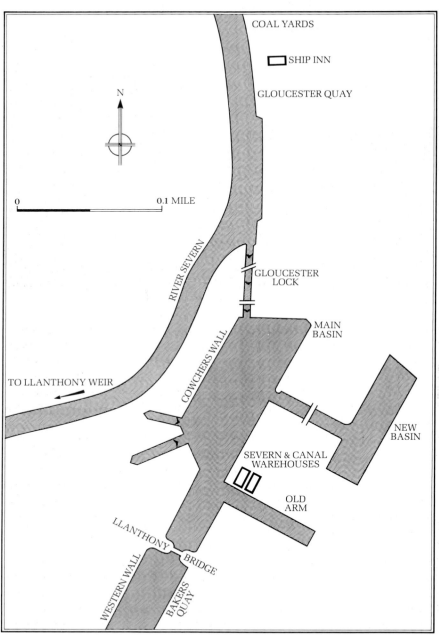

COAL YARDS

SHIP INN

GLOUCESTER QUAY

N

0          0.1 MILE

RIVER SEVERN

GLOUCESTER
LOCK

MAIN
BASIN

TO LLANTHONY WEIR

COWCHERS WALL

NEW
BASIN

SEVERN & CANAL
WAREHOUSES

OLD
ARM

LLANTHONY
BRIDGE

WESTERN WALL

BAKERS QUAY

Gloucester Docks and the Riverside Quay

Loading a longboat from a barge in the Old Arm at Gloucester

barge coming up the canal, they'd want two boats to be alongside her at 8 o'clock the next morning and others a bit later. For a barge moored under the ton crane in front of the company's warehouse, you usually laid in loose between the barge and the quay, and you pushed the boat along as you loaded each part. A motor barge had its own derrick, and so could also load another boat on the outside. Around the corner was a double derrick on the quay, and one jib of this could load a boat lying between the barge and the quay while the other was loading a boat outside the barge.

For bagged stuff, you filled a quarter of the hold without moving the boat. Each bag was lowered on to a staging rigged from the side of the barge, and one of the crew of the barge took off the hoisting rope. The skipper was in the longboat, and he caught hold of each sack, carried it a short distance and dropped it down just where it had to go. Normally it didn't matter which part of the hold was loaded first, but if a check under the false floors showed the boat was leaking, he started loading the middle part first to keep the boat level. If he started at one end, the boat would have gone down unevenly, and the water could have spoiled the first lot of cargo loaded. When they had filled one quarter of the hold, the skipper moved the boat along so they could load another quarter and then the other two.

He knew how many bags he had to put in each section so that the boat finished up properly trimmed. It was usual to have the boat a little down by the head – if it was down by the stern, it wouldn't steer properly. Also this meant that the skipper could check if the boat was leaking by lifting the deck lid and seeing how much water was inside. A good man could stow 300 2¼-cwt sacks in a longboat in an hour and fifteen minutes. Some tried to beat that time and they prided themselves on how fast they could do it. Others didn't hurry so much and, if they wanted a break, there was often a spectator who would carry some. Young chaps of sixteen or seventeen thought it was a really good thing to have a go at sack carrying.

If you were loading copper or cased goods, the skipper had to keep under the crane because he couldn't carry that stuff. They used to send up ten cases at a time on a sling and lower them into the boat. He put them into stacks, released the sling and soon there was another ten waiting for him to do. Before loading heavy cargoes like steel plates or copper 'cigars', he laid out some dunnage for the cargo to rest on and let the hoist chains pass underneath. It was the skipper's responsibility to load his boat safely, and he knew how much he could carry. With a heavy cargo, he went to a maximum of 33 tons – 300 sacks of wheat or 360 bags of sugar. Carbide was in 1- or 2-cwt drums and barrels of glucose weighed 4 cwt. With copper, there were so many bars or slabs to the ton, and pieces of spelter [zinc] were ½-cwt each. A checker counted everything on to the boat and wrote down what you were having.

With a bulky cargo, the load was limited by what you could fit under the cloths. Light cargoes were stacked right up to the planks nearly all the way along, with only a little space left behind the mast so there was somewhere to put the horse's corn. With a very light cargo, like cornflakes, a boat was inclined to roll, so when possible a heavier cargo like copper or spelter was put in the bottom of the boat to keep it stable. For loading a long cargo like timber or steel it was necessary to get out the beams that went across the hold, but when the boat was loaded the sides were pushed in a bit and it was difficult to get the beams back in 'again. So each beam had a groove in the end that you could fit a crowbar into, and you stood on the beam and used the crowbar to force the side of the boat out, allowing the beam to fall into place.

As the skipper stowed the cargo, the mate usually set up the planks and put the cloths on. He pulled up the side cloths and put all the strings over to tie them up, and then he opened out the big top cloths that had been piled on the foredeck. Along the top, he put a width of canvas called a tippet to protect the top cloths from being cut by the top strings and from being damaged when you ran along the planks. When carrying timber, the planks and top cloths were not needed as it was sufficient to stack the wood up level and only have the side cloths tied across the top.

Once he'd finished loading, the skipper went to the office, picked up all his papers and drew his starting money. He was given a trip note saying what tonnage was being carried, where to, how much a ton and how much driving money [when empty]. The skipper also had a consignment note saying what the cargo was – so many sacks of this or cases of that etc. He had to get this note signed by the receiver and bring it back to the office when collecting the rest of his money.

While the skipper was at the office, the mate moved the boat over to Cowchers Wall [the West Quay]. The crew of the barge had a line off the stern of the boat, and they pulled her along the length of their barge. This usually gave the boat just enough way to go across to the other side by Cowcher's Warehouses, but if the pump in the engine house over that side was working to top up the level of the canal, the water was in a swirl and the boat would stop in the middle. So the mate had to take the

Loaded longboats in the Main Basin at Gloucester

boat further up the dock and wait for the skipper to help him across where the water was quieter. Once on Cowcher's Wall, you usually moored there for the night. But if there were more than six boats, which was the most that could fit in the lock together, they locked some down into the river that afternoon, and you had to bow-haul your boat along the riverside Quay and tie up opposite the Ship Inn.

To get water when moored by the lock, you took your water can to the tap facing the Dock Office entrance. You had to press the tap to make it work and hold it there until the can was full. If you were moored at the Quay, you could get water from a tap near the old Ship Inn. This water was kept for drinking, and you used it carefully because if you ran out, you might have to go a long way until you got to the next lock-keeper where you could ask for some more.

The next morning, you were towed up the river by one of the tugs owned by the Severn and Canal Carrying Company. These operated a regular service – one leaving Gloucester every morning bound for Worcester and crossing with another returning from the previous day. In the 1920s, this service was provided by three steam tugs, *Active, Victor* and *Alert* and if there was a lot of traffic, another tug was sometimes provided by the Dock Company. *Active* and *Victor* were both built in 1904 by G.K. Stothert and Company at Bristol, and they were well-suited to the work. In the early days, the crew comprised the captain, mate, engineer and fireman, although later they only had three men. There were bunks in the fore-end for the crew, and the captain had a cabin by himself aft. The helmsman had to stand out in the open. There was a canvas awning he could fix up, supported by iron bars, but it didn't really keep him dry if there was a strong wind blowing the rain underneath.

*Alert* was a much older tug, built in 1886 by Finch and Company of Chepstow. She had a high pressure cylinder on top of the low pressure one [tandem compound], and as she only had one crank, it sometimes used to stick at top dead centre. I remember once they tried to go astern to stop as they went into Gloucester Lock, but it didn't work and they ran into the gates! Also her valve gear was above the cylinders and never encased because they thought they wouldn't be keeping her. If there was any fresh water in the river, there was a risk the valve gear wouldn't get under the bridges. This was considered a bit dangerous, and so she was only used when it was really necessary. Before the First World War, *Athlete* had also been in service, but the traffic had diminished and she was broken up during the 1920s.

Steam tug *Alert* at Gloucester

Severn and Canal had a coal yard on the riverside Quay at Gloucester, and the tugs picked up coal there almost every time they returned. A tug could carry about 2½ tons of coal, but sometimes it was also piled up on the deck because if they had light tows, they could then have sufficient for two trips. At night, the tug moored beside the river Quay, and the crew banked up the fire by putting plenty of slack on. Next morning, they used their long fork to turn the fire over until it burned up again, and then they drifted down backwards with the current to meet the boats locking down from the basin. As the gates opened, they got the stern of the tug in the lock's mouth right by the boats, and they handed out a heavy towing rope to each boat.

The special ropes were more than twice as long as a boat and had an eye on each end. The rope from the boat in front was put on to one of the timberheads near the bow, and the rope to the boat behind was put on to the same timberhead. This left each boat's stern end free to turn in one direction, but if the helm was put over the other way, the rope wouldn't let her swing far. Leaving Gloucester, the ropes went down the right-hand side of the boats so each boat's stern was free to swing when going out of the lock. Otherwise, if one boat was pushed over to the left by the current going down to the weir, he'd pull the next one over more, and the last one could get stuck across the river. Once the ropes were hitched on, away went the tug with all the boats in order according to their turn. If there were any boats waiting at the Quay, they would catch on behind.

In the summer, a steam tug could take up to ten or twelve longboats, but rather less in the winter when the river current was stronger. One summer when the river was low, *Active* had sixteen longboats, and it took two days to get to Worcester. They talked about it for years! The first day, they went as far as Upton upon Severn and the next day from Upton upon Severn to Worcester. But the engineer and the fireman said they wouldn't do it again – they didn't get any rest for fourteen hours. The tugs also towed any barges or timber lighters going to Tewkesbury or Worcester, but then they took less longboats. The barges went first on the tug with the boats following in one or two lines behind.

Going up the river, the steerers had to keep alert or they could cause difficulties for other boats in the tow. There was a sharp turn to the right to go under Westgate Bridge, and this was another reason for the ropes being on the right side of each boat, leaving the stern free to turn away from the rope. However, each boat cut the corner a bit more than the one in front and, unless the steering was just right, the last boats in a long tow couldn't avoid rubbing the bank. The next bend was to the left, and each boat had to keep to the right of the one in front so that the ropes did not restrict steerage. The tug skipper knew he had to keep out from the right bank, or the last boat would rub the trees. This meant losing a bit of time because he was more in the current, but it was worth it to keep going with no upsets. If your longboat veered towards the right bank, you did your best to shove the tiller over, but as your stern came across the rope of the boat behind, it pulled that boat towards the bank and the next boat behind as well. The more you pushed the tiller over, the more you were bearing on his rope, and you weren't helping at all to keep him away from the bank. He usually got out of it, but it was something you tried not to let happen.

The worst turn on the river was going out of the Parting where the other channel of the river runs down to Maisemore. This required a right turn, and it was another reason to have the ropes on the right side of each boat. The tug kept in the slack water close to the right bank and, if there was any fresh water in the river, it was vital for the boats to follow round behind. If one boat started to wander out, he could get caught in the current going down to Maisemore and the sideways pull of the rope could turn him over. Or the next boat could catch up, causing a slack rope, and then as the tug moved forward, if the rope came out of the water with a jerk, it could break. If this happened, it was every man for himself because you were heading for Maisemore Weir! You'd turn your boat hard into the bank, jump ashore with a rope and lash it round a tree or something. Each one that was behind you would do the same, and each one would hold his boat there until the tug dropped back, gave you another rope and off you'd go again.

When I started as a boy, I was often left to steer up the river while the skipper made a meal or had a nap. You were supposed to keep the boat into the slacks close to the bank so the tug could gain all the time she could, and if you let the boat run out into the current, the captain of the tug might 'Toot Toot'. Your skipper didn't like that, particularly if he was asleep in the cabin, and you'd get a back-hander! They never used to warn you first, so you soon learned to keep the boat straight and not to run off.

Approaching Tewkesbury Lock, the tug kept going until she was well into the lock. In so doing, she gave enough way for the first two boats to go up by the tug, and most of the others drifted on into the lock. If a boatman could get his hook-shaft against the lock gate he pulled himself in. If he couldn't reach the gates, he could try putting the shaft in the water to shove the boat along, but the shaft would probably go into mud. So sometimes a lock-keeper would throw a line and help pull the last boats in. Occasionally, one or two boats had to pull themselves in using the tow ropes. The tug tied up to the top gates and then all the boats could pull in their ropes to get the last boat into the lock. This was something that could not be rushed, and if one of the last boats pulled before the others were secure, there were shouts of 'Don't pull yet, you . . . you're pulling me back!' In the lock, the boats were just left loose with most of the ropes trailing in the water, although the last boats pulled their ropes up to prevent them getting caught under the bottom gates. Also the ropes were changed over to the left-hand side of the boats to help them turn left into the main current when going out of the lock cutting.

Going on up the river, if *Active* or *Victor* had a big tow, they sometimes ran out of steam. Then the mate shouted 'Turn 'em in,' and all the boats had to turn in to the bank and hang on to the nearest tree or bush. They cleared the fires, and you'd hang on there maybe 10 or 15 minutes until they got a good head of steam back on. *Alert* had a better boiler, and she very rarely had to turn in for steam.

Steam tug *Active* and longboats at Ryall Bank near Upton upon Severn. The lightly loaded boat is on a short rope to help steering

At Diglis, near Worcester, you normally went in the big barge lock because that would take the tug and six boats. If there were more boats in the tow, the last ones had to cast off and go up into the small boat lock. They went in the cutting all right, but then each skipper had to use his shaft to push against the bank. As they neared the lock, the lock-keeper usually threw them a line and pulled them in until they could get a hook-shaft on to the gate. If the lock-keeper was too busy to help, one of the boatmen put his shaft into a hard bit of the bank and jumped across carrying a line so he could bow-haul the boat into the lock.

In Diglis Lock, the ropes were rearranged in preparation for getting the boats into the barge lock at the entrance to the Worcester and Birmingham Canal. At the same time, they sent someone ahead to get the entrance lock ready. The first two boats were tied abreast on a short rope behind the tug, and the next two were on a longer rope from another hook. As they approached the wide entrance lock, the tug slowed down and the first two boats shot off straight into the lock under their own speed. Then the tug moved forward again, and the second two boats went alongside the wall just above the lock entrance and put a

Severn and Canal boats entering the Worcester and Birmingham Canal at Worcester

rope ashore. As soon as the lock was clear, the second pair drifted back slowly with the current and they were then pulled into the lock. If there was a lot of fresh in the river, the tug helped with this operation – otherwise it went back to bring up any remaining boats. To cast off from the tug, you had to chuck the heavy tow-rope off the timberhead, and sometimes this got stuck – particularly if the eye of the rope was wet and the timberhead was badly scored. So the mate of the tug always stood by the slip hook, which had a catch over the top with a pin through, and if necessary he pulled the pin out and let the rope fly off. Then you coiled the rope up on the lock wall and left it for the tug to pick up later. Boats going to Stourport tied up in the cutting just outside Diglis Lock, and they waited there until the Stourport tug came down next morning.

# CHAPTER 3

# *Into the Midlands*

*The most common route for the longboats to go into the Midlands was up the Worcester and Birmingham Canal to Bournville and Birmingham. The other route up the Staffordshire and Worcestershire Canal to Wolverhampton and Walsall is described later.*

Coming up on the tug from Gloucester, you usually arrived at Worcester late in the afternoon, but it could be earlier if there were only a few other boats with you or later if there was a lot of fresh water in the river. There are two barge locks to get up from the river into Diglis Basin, and the longboats worked up through these in pairs. Usually you started off up the canal that evening if there was a horse available. While the boat was rising in the lock, you picked up two sacks of corn from Severn and Canal's own stable, took them on the sack truck back to the boat and put them underneath the cloths. There was a bale of hay if you wanted one, but most didn't bother about it because they could get hay at the stables up the canal. Then you fetched the horse from the stable and, as you walked him round the basin, the skipper bow-hauled the boat out of the lock with enough speed to get across the basin and meet you at the start of the canal. When you brought the horse, the skipper threw you the line, you pegged him to and away you went up the canal towards Birmingham.

You looked forward to stopping about 7 or 8 o'clock according to where the next stable was for your horse. You might want to carry on up the canal, but in the evening the lock-keepers put a chain and padlock on one pair of gates in each flight so you couldn't go any further. If somebody neglected to drop a paddle and didn't close a gate properly, the water could be running all night and one of the pounds could be drained. Then they'd have to run water from a reservoir in the morning to fill up the pound again. To avoid this, the lock-keepers made sure that all was done right in the evening, and then they put the padlocks on. So you had to choose where to stop for the night before they locked up or else your horse might not get a stable. You found out off the other boatmen where they were going to stop and who was going to start when in the morning, and then there was no arguments about losing turns.

When you used a stable at a pub, they charged you a shilling or sixpence, and they gave you a little ticket as a receipt. When you got back to Gloucester, you handed the piece of paper in at the office, and they gave you the money for it. At some pubs, if you went in to have a drink, they gave you a ticket without you paying anything. It was a way of getting custom, and in return you cleaned the stable out before you left next morning.

If you came up late, you had to moor in the basin at Worcester overnight. After about 7 o'clock, the stableman wouldn't let you have a horse, and you had to wait until he opened the stable in the morning and the locks were unlocked at about 7 o'clock. The first two canal locks are deep and narrow and, if a boat got jammed, it could take a long time to get through. So you always tried to get above the Blockhouse Lock if you could. There was a five-horse stable there belonging to the pub, the Lame Dog, and then you had a nice comfortable pull up to Tardebigge the next day. When you stopped above the Blockhouse, you could be away at 5·30, and you were clear until Sammy Wareings, which was the eighth lock from Diglis Basin. Usually, he had taken the chain off by the time you got there, and then you were well on your way. Even with a big full load, you could make Tardebigge by about 5 or 6 o'clock at night, and there was no need to rush the horse. But when several boats stopped above the Blockhouse, the pound would be down because it was one lock of water gone for each boat, and unless there was something coming over the weirs in the night, you were scraping along the bottom in the morning, particularly by the railway bridge where it was very shallow.

If you had reached Worcester in good time, you'd go on further up the canal. There were stables at Blackpole, Gilbert's Lock before the Five Mile Pound, Tibberton Bridge, Hanbury Wharf and Stoke. You'd go on no matter how dark or icy it was. At night, the canal shows up like a silver streak and you can even see the horse on the tow-path. The further you went, the easier it was for the horse the next day. In the morning, you usually started as soon as the lock-keeper took the chain off, but it was possible to get away earlier if you were in a real hurry. To

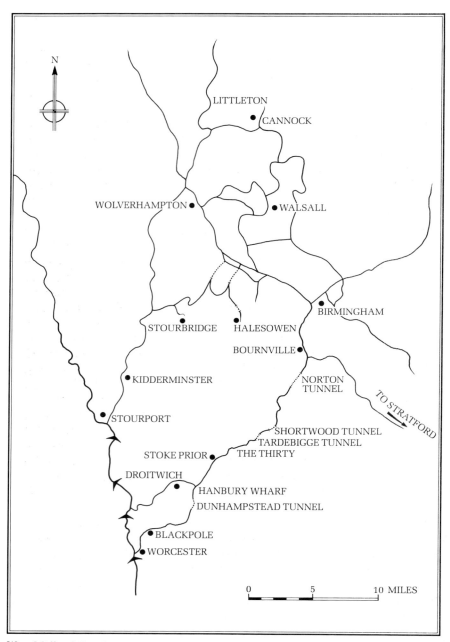

LITTLETON

● CANNOCK

WOLVERHAMPTON ●

● WALSALL

● BIRMINGHAM

STOURBRIDGE    HALESOWEN

BOURNVILLE ●

● KIDDERMINSTER

NORTON
TUNNEL

TO STRATFORD

● STOURPORT

SHORTWOOD TUNNEL
TARDEBIGGE TUNNEL
THE THIRTY

STOKE PRIOR ●

DROITWICH

HANBURY WHARF
DUNHAMPSTEAD TUNNEL

● BLACKPOLE

● WORCESTER

0          5          10 MILES

West Midland Canals

stop the locks being used in the evening, the lock-keeper wound half a paddle up and put a chain through the wheel. To overcome this, you used a piece of canvas weighted with bricks to cover the paddle hole, and then you worked the lock very quietly before the lock-keeper got up so he never knew how you did it!

Soon after leaving Worcester, you passed Cadbury's factory at Blackpole where they made boxes and also stored raw materials. Then after several more locks, you came to the Five Mile Pound. This was a good place to catch eels because there was a lot of salt in the water coming down from the salt-works at Stoke Prior. You could dip a net over the bow of a loaded boat or use an eel spear and just plunge it into the reeds at random as you went along.

Some way along the Five Mile Pound is Dunhampstead Tunnel [236 yd] where the boat had to be pulled through using one of the hand rails running along each side. Approaching the tunnel, you gave the horse a bit of a gee-up to give the boat a good start, and the horse kept pulling as long as he could. As the line caught on the tunnel entrance, the luby on top of the mast was supposed to bend back letting the line fly off. But sometimes the rope had slipped down below the bulge in the luby which then held the line, and the result was that both the boat and the horse were brought up short! Once in the tunnel, the steerer stood on the fore-end and pulled the boat through. He kept to the left going up loaded because that was the deepest side of the tunnel. The horse had to go up over the top of the tunnel. When you got to the other end, just over the opening was a weight fixed on a bit of chain so it couldn't fall. You lowered the end of the rope down in front of the opening and put the weight on the rope to hold it in position. Then you took the horse along the tow-path a bit and waited. As the boat came out of the tunnel, the man on the fore-end caught hold of the line and put it on the mast. Then you started the horse moving forward, the rope pulled clear from underneath the weight and away you'd go.

Towards the end of the Five Mile Pound was Hanbury Wharf, where you sometimes took a part cargo for a small mill. Also, it was a stopping place because there was a pub there and you put your horse in the stable. After six more locks, you passed Stoke Prior Salt Works and then on to Stoke Wharf where there was a shop. You took enough food with you from Gloucester to last a couple of days, but if you wanted something extra, you'd go to the shop while the boat was rising in the lock. You tried to be back by the time the lock was full, but that wasn't always possible. Nearby was a tap where you could fill your water can.

Longboat climbing up towards the reservoir on the Tardebigge flight

After the Stoke locks, you went round a corner and you saw the Thirty rising up almost like a flight of stairs – thirty locks in two miles! To help work the locks, some of the older boatmen employed men known as hobblers who were waiting at Hanbury and Tardebigge. They'd do forty-two locks for two shillings, and they used to sleep rough – it was slavery. About halfway up the locks was the Halfway House Farm which was also a pub. We used to take a jug and get some milk there for a penny a pint.

After going up the Thirty, you usually spent the second night at Tardebigge and went through the tunnels on the summit level when the tug started work in the morning. But if you could get as far as Hanbury Wharf on the first night, you could be at Tardebigge to catch the midday tug and then get through to Birmingham for the second night. One tug towed through Tardebigge and Shortwood Tunnels [568 and 608 yd], another towed through Kings Norton Tunnel [2,726 yd] and a spare tug was kept in the depot at Tardebigge in case she was wanted. As several boats would go through on one tug, the horses were taken over the top in a group, and this was usually a job for the children. It was a good time to hang a feed of corn on them while they were just walking, but some children took the opportunity of riding the horses, and where the path crossed a field, they had a race to the other side.

Before a tug entered a tunnel, the crew got up a full head of steam. Although there were two air shafts in the tunnel, they knew they mustn't fire-up too much while going through or they'd choke you. After Tardebigge Tunnel, the tug continued to tow, and they fired up ready for Shortwood Tunnel. If it was late in the afternoon and you wanted to save a bit of time, you might also get the horses to help pull between these two tunnels. As you came out of Shortwood Tunnel, the boats cast off and the tug swung round in the winding hole ready for going back to Tardebigge. From there to the entrance to Norton Tunnel, the horses pulled the boats again, and then there was another tug for Norton Tunnel. They usually had to fire up in this much longer tunnel, and they did so a bit at a time so it would burn quickly and keep a bright fire. Even so, there was so much smoke you couldn't see a thing and some of the boatmen couldn't stand it. When you got to the Birmingham end, the tug went into her lie-bye and let the boats go by. Then you could go through to Birmingham on the level, and you could keep going faster than when you were climbing the locks.

Approaching Birmingham, the nearness of the railway could cause

Boats at the entrance to King's Norton Tunnel

trouble if you had a fresh horse or an army mule that had been in shell-shock. If a train went by, you had to go to his head. There were coping stones all along the canal into Birmingham, and some were sloping down into the canal. If a horse slipped there, he could go right in, and you might have to walk a mile or more to find somewhere shallow to get him out. Two horses I knew were drowned because of this. There's a long railway bridge as you go through Selly Oak, and one time our mule was frightened by a train there and I couldn't hold him. His back legs went off and in he went. The skipper shouted at me and the skies were blue! I kept the mule's head up while the skipper stripped the boat. Then he used the planks to lever the mule up, and inch by inch we pulled him out. He had cut legs and sores, but he managed it to Birmingham. The vet put some stuff on, and we had to stop there for a couple of days until he was all right to return.

Approaching Gas Street Basin in Birmingham, there is a very sharp turn called the Muck Turn because it was beside the Corporation Refuse Depot. Then if you were discharging at Gas Street, you tied up first beside the tow-path on the left and put your horse in the stable there. You didn't usually stay alongside the tow-path overnight because there were thugs about then and they could cut your cloths and take your cargo while you were asleep. So you moored beside the Bar which ran across the basin, and there could be four or five boats there waiting to unload. Sometimes boats from other companies, such as Fellows Morton and Clayton, moored on the other side of the Bar as it was closer for them to go up the steps and into town.

When you had discharged, you went to the Severn and Canal office in Bridge Street and asked whether they had any load to go back. Usually there was nothing, and so you took the boat back to Gloucester empty – a day from Birmingham down to Worcester, and the next day from Worcester on the tug to Gloucester. Coming home empty, you didn't usually cloth up. You took the cratch down and stood it in the front of the hold and you put the fore-cloth over the dunnage to keep it all dry. To avoid the false bottoms getting wet, you could stack them up in the middle of the boat and put a bit of canvas over them too. You had the planks resting on the beams so it was easier to run along them. If you slipped off, you'd only go into the bottom of the boat, whereas if you slipped off when you were clothed up, you'd be in the water.

When several boats were coming back to Worcester, it was the first to get to Diglis Basin that was first on turn, and the first on turn at Worcester was first on the tug and first to load again when he got back to

Severn and Canal boats moored beside the Bar at Gas Street Basin in Birmingham

Gloucester. The order of boats was usually fixed at Norton Tunnel, because coming down the Thirty you couldn't overtake anything, and even on the Five Mile Pound the boats were well spaced out because of the time needed to work through the previous lock. Only if a boat stopped early for the night did he risk losing his turn. If you wanted to keep ahead and hold your turn, you kept ploughing along no matter how dark it was until the locks were locked up.

You usually spent the night in the basin at Worcester and then took the boat out on to the river in the morning. In the early days, you had to bow-haul the longboats from the bottom lock of the Worcester and Birmingham Canal down to Diglis Lock. The first two boats waited in the pound above the bottom lock for the tug to go by from its mooring near Worcester Bridge. The tugmen didn't stop to give you a pull into the cutting – that was against their principles in those days. The only help they gave was two blasts on the hooter as if to say 'We shall be waiting for you in the lock.' When leaving the bottom lock, the mate had to shove the boat out as far as he could and then steer to keep her away from the bank. The skipper took the rope and pulled his heart out to get a start, and then he had to get his feet going a bit to keep ahead of the current.

If there was a lot of fresh water in the river, you'd get a horse from the stable, and he could manage two boats abreast as long as they were empty. When the boats came out of the bottom lock, they were heading downstream for the weir. So you set up the line and started to drive the horse as fast as he could go depending on the current. As soon as the boats reached the lock cutting, they were in still water, and the line could be let go leaving the boats to drift on down to the lock. Then you took the horse back and maybe brought two more boats down. Meanwhile, the tug was waiting in the lock, and the crew were idling about drinking tea. All you got from them was 'How much longer are you going to be?' But things were to change. By the 1930s, the boatmen wouldn't pull their boats any more, and the tug had to take them wherever they had to go.

Sometimes in the early days, instead of coming straight down the canal to Worcester, you'd turn off at Hanbury Wharf and go down to Droitwich to pick up a load of salt. Then you went on down the Droitwich Canal and joined the Severn just above Bevere Lock. Getting out of the Droitwich Canal was tricky because you had to get across the River Severn to the other side before you were carried over Bevere Weir. Leaving the lock, one of the crew got a rope on the stern and pulled as hard as he could and, as the boat came to the end of the lock, he jumped on board. At the same time, the other member of the crew was on the bow pushing with a Severn shaft against the bank to force the bow up against the stream. A Severn shaft was a long heavy shaft with two straight prongs on the end. You shot across as far as you could, and then you used the shaft again to get the boat into the side so you could jump ashore like pole vaulting. You took a rope ashore with you, and you kept the boat close into the bank going down into the lock. You only did this when you knew a tug was on its way down from Stourport, and it would pick you up in the lock.

Coming down the river behind the tug, the boats were usually empty which made them difficult to steer, and so they were tied two abreast on short ropes. The first two were close up to the tug, each with a rope from the tug's hook, and the boats behind were on cross ropes from the sterns of the boats in front. Then it didn't matter whether the tug went straight or round a corner, all the boats had to follow. This meant you didn't have to steer, and you spent the time cleaning your cabin or talking to your friends. But if there was a loaded boat in the tow, he was on a long rope at the back, and he did have to steer.

Most boatmen took a pride in keeping their cabin clean, and every-thing had to come out and be scrubbed – including the clothes drawer

Going downstream towards Gloucester. The loaded boat is on a long rope

and the table cupboard. You cleaned the brasses and sandstoned the bare woodwork, like the gunnels round the hatches, which had too much wear to be painted. You even cleaned the coal-box until it was as white as paper. While you were doing this, the coal had to be put on the hatches, and when you put it back in the box, you had to sandstone the floor it had been on. Some boats had oak gunnels which came up brown, so at Stourport you asked for them to be replaced by ash which came up white. A piece of canvas was often fixed underneath the gunnels so it could be put over the top to provide protection during the working day and then hung down at night to show the wood again. When you got to Gloucester Quay, the tug just snapped his hook to release the tow rope, and someone had to jump ashore with a stern line from the last boat. Then each boat was bow-hauled into the lock while the tug turned round and went back to moor by the coal yard.

When the river level was high, it was difficult coming down through the bridges just above Gloucester. Westgate Bridge had a low arch, and the boats had to keep in the middle or the slope of the arch could rip the cabin off. Also the Black Bridge [railway] had a pillar jutting out into the river, and the current could knock the boat into that if you weren't careful. So if you were worried about going through fast behind the tug, you'd cast off before the bridges and drop down backwards trailing a pig. A pig was a piece of iron weighing about 1 cwt with a ring in the middle, and you had it ready across the foredeck already shackled into the eye of your farling. This rope was coiled carefully, starting from the outside and coming in, so when you threw the pig off, the rope wouldn't foul up. With the pig dragging along the bottom, the boat swung round to point upstream, and the rudder had some steerage effect as the water rushed past it. In this way, you could drop down slowly through the bridges and round the corner to Gloucester Quay.

In the early days, the river tugs didn't work on Sundays. So if you got to Worcester on Saturday and the tug had gone, rather than wait until Monday morning, you just drifted down the river to Gloucester. Mostly you came down in pairs so the two crews could help one another. If the boats drifted close to the bank, you used the Severn shaft to push against the bottom of the river, or if you were going against the trees, you could push it against a branch. Another thing we did was to lash shovels on to the end of two shafts and use them as big sculls for a bit. Coming under Mythe Bridge, we got over to the side away from Tewkesbury because the lock was on that side and we didn't want to go with the main river over the weir. To help get round the bend approaching the lock, someone jumped off with a line, and he did a bit of bow-hauling to keep the boat close to the bank until it went into the lock. Similarly approaching the Parting, someone got ashore with a line to pull the boats into the Gloucester water.

Whenever there was a bit of wind blowing down the river, we fixed up a sail. We tied one of the planks up against the mast and put a block at the top with a rope through. For the sail, we used one of the cloths meant for covering the cargo, and we tied a shaft across at the top and one at the bottom. Then we hoisted the sail up to the block on the mast and had two bits of rope from the bottom corners to pull it round to catch the wind. The sail helped us along so well, you could hear the water rippling behind the stern. Normally though we just drifted, and it took a long time.

Once back at Gloucester, the skipper took his papers into the Severn and Canal office and collected the balance of his pay. Then he went back home and waited his turn for another trip. The average time waiting was a few days, but you could be tied up for a couple of weeks, and during that time you signed on for the dole. Occasionally, the company gave you a casual job with a sack truck or on the guy rope pulling the jib of the derrick over, but this wasn't common.

While waiting for their turns, most of the crews went back to their own homes in Gloucester, but when I started on the boats as a boy, I didn't have a home to go to. So when I returned from a trip, if there wasn't another skipper to go with, I had to rough it. For shelter at night, I got in under the cloths of a loaded boat with a couple of empty sacks. I crawled inside one of them up to my shoulders, folded the other over for a pillow and there I was for the night. If there was no loaded boat, I'd get into an empty boat where the fore-end of the hold was covered by the cratch. For food, I had to earn a crust of bread where I could. One possible job was to clean out a spare boat before it was used. If a regular boat had to go into dock at Stourport for overhaul, the skipper took over a spare boat that was kept at the top of the Old Arm. If there was no other work about, I was glad to clean it for ten shillings – there was a couple of steaks in that! Usually though, I had to collect jam jars or rabbit skins that had been chucked in the rubbish and take them to sell. Or I'd collect empty tins and melt them down for the solder – anything to get a few bob to have something to eat. What a life!

*Although the majority of trips for Severn and Canal longboats made use of the Worcester and Birmingham Canal, it was also common to go up the river to Stourport, then up the Staffordshire and Worcestershire Canal and on to Wolverhampton and Walsall.*

The Gloucester tug took the boats to Worcester and, in the early 1920s, there was a special little steam tug called *Pioneer* that did the Worcester to Stourport run. For a few years, *Mistletoe* replaced *Pioneer*, but after 1926 the Gloucester tugs did the full length whenever needed. To get up into the basins at Stourport, there are two pairs of narrow locks, and the boats were worked through by bow-hauling. Then from the first basin, you had to get the boat into the middle basin and on up to Cottons Lock by a combination of pulling with a line and pushing with a shaft. There wasn't room for the horse to pull until you got to the lock.

Severn and Canal didn't have a proper stable at Stourport, so you usually had to get a horse from Worcester and take him to Stourport. He was tackled up ready for work, and you were not supposed to ride him, although the children often did in spite of getting a sore backside. You didn't go up the river tow-path as it was quicker to go by the road. So you went through the heart of Worcester, past the cathedral, and out into the country. At Ombersley, about half-way to Stourport, there was a little house where you could sit down and have a cup of tea, and then you went on past the Mitre Oak to Stourport. You got there long before

Steam tug and longboats passing under Holt Bridge

the tug, so you could put the horse in the stable by the Tontine public house, and you might have time to walk down to Lincomb Lock and meet the boat there. On the return journey, you had to walk all the way again to bring the horse back to Worcester, and you had to start an hour before the tug to get to Worcester in time. Just occasionally, you could leave the horse at Stourport if they knew there was another boat on the way up the river that needed it.

We didn't like the Staffordshire and Worcestershire Canal because it was shallow, and you could get stuck on the mud on the bottom. We used to lighten the cargo down to 30 tons at Stourport, but even then the horse couldn't always pull the boat up the canal. I've seen a horse winded trying to pull a boat along, and I've spent a night stuck in the middle of a pound. The horse had to do without a stable that night – all we could do was put a canvas cloth over him and just stand him under the hedge. Fortunately, there was a good flow into the canal from a sewage works near Autherley Junction, and this usually made the weirs run during the night. We waited until the water rose enough, and then the horse had another go in the morning.

Also there were several sharp bends that you had a job to get round because of the mud. You were only doing about two miles an hour with a horse boat, and you hadn't got a lot of steerage on the rudder, so you banged the helm over repeatedly, using the rudder like an oar, to try to get the stern to go over. If the tow-path was on the inside of the bend, you sometimes had to put the line on the stud and try to pull her round with the horse. If the tow-path was on the outside, you threw a line ashore from the stern to help pull the stern round. Because of these difficulties, you couldn't work to a time. If the canal level was up, you'd go from Stourport to Wolverhampton with a loaded boat in about 16 hr, but if the water was low, you could be two days trying to get through the muck.

On the Staffordshire and Worcestershire Canal, they never used to lock up any of the locks, and so if the water was well up, you could start at 5 o'clock in the morning and go on well after dark. Sometimes you had a fly night and didn't stop at all. If there was a boat coming behind you, the skipper wasn't going to loose his turn or the other boat would get his cargo there before you, and there might not be any room for your cargo. So you did everything you could to stop him catching you, and if necessary you kept walking all night. You had the light on the canal from the sky, and it was never so dark that the horse didn't know his way – all you had to do was to hold on to him!

Longboats waiting for the tug below the Tontine Hotel at Stourport

At Aldersley Junction, you started the big climb up to Wolverhampton – twenty-one locks in two miles! Going on to Walsall, you turned off on to the Wyrley and Essington Canal and then on to the Bentley Canal. You went down six locks and another four, and then there was a sharp bend to join the Walsall Canal. If there was a stoppage while you were at Walsall, you could go up the Walsall locks and come back round the Wyrley. Returning empty, you came down the Staffordshire and Worcestershire Canal much quicker than going up. Then at Stourport, you went out on to the river and waited for the tug just below the Tontine pub. When you arrived at Stourport, you had your note signed to record the time, and this fixed your turn compared with the boats coming down to Worcester. But if you came down after the office closed, they had to take your word for the time, and this sometimes led to arguments and even fights when you got back to Gloucester.

# CHAPTER 4

# *Working Horse Boats*

*The Severn and Canal Carrying Company had its own stable at Worcester that could cater for over thirty horses, and there were also some hospital stalls for sick animals.*

After the First World War, the company had a lot of army horses and mules which were very cheap, but some had been in shell-shock and were difficult to handle. A good horse knew what he had to do and could be a great help to the efficient working of the boat. If you had a good one, you'd ask the stableman to let you have him again, but usually you didn't get any choice as he gave them out in the order they came back from their previous trip. Sometimes there were that many boats going up the canal that you had to wait for a horse to return from Birmingham, and then he had to have a rest before you could take him back out. The Canal Company also had a small stable at Worcester for donkeys that could be hired by owners who didn't have their own horses, but Severn and Canal boats didn't usually use these.

When tackled for work, the horse had ropes running back from his collar on either side and passing through bobbins to avoid chafing his body. Behind the horse was a wooden spreader, and then the ropes joined together further back in a loop to which the end of the boat line was attached. Instead of a spreader, some horses had a swingle tree, which was a stronger piece of wood with a hook in the middle, and the end of the boat line went directly on to the hook. To use this, you had to come up close behind his back legs, so it wasn't fitted on a horse which kicked.

The rope you attached to the horse to pull a longboat was called a cut line. It was pure cotton, as thick as your finger, and about 80 ft long. The weight of the whole line was 7 lb – they wouldn't allow you to use anything heavier, and if you did, you could get an inspector on you for overweighting the horse. Some boatmen saved a few bob and used a 6-lb line, which was softer but didn't wear as well. On one end of the line was an eye splice to fit on the luby on top of the mast, and splicing was one of the first things you were taught to do. You'd get a small bit of rope with three strands, and you'd go on practising until you got it right. You opened the strands with your fingers, pushed the ends through and drew them tight, but very often you had to pull it out and have another go. You didn't use a marline-spike with cotton lines because they were always soft when new. Spliced into the other end of the cut line was a peg about 3 or 4 in long made from a good heavy broom handle. This was attached to the horse's tackle by pushing it through the loop at the back and turning it sideways. Then if necessary, you could unhitch it quickly.

If you were careful, a line would last three or maybe four trips, but if you had a keen horse, it might only last two-and-a-half trips. There were certain bridges where the tow-path came sharp round and the rope made great cuts into the brickwork because the boat was still coming round the corner. On some of these, the brickwork was protected by a piece of iron, but the ropes even cut grooves in that. If the line went into a previous groove, it would run round smoothly, but if it caught the sharp edge between two grooves, it would be cut. Also the line could be damaged if it got squeezed between the boat and the side of a lock. The boatman had to pay for the cut line, so you treated it like gold and prayed you didn't have a mad horse! Some horses went up the stretch so hard, you thought they'd pull the mast out of the boat. You tried to hold them back, but sometimes you weren't strong enough and they bust the line. If you knew the line was worn and you could afford it, you bought a second one and put it in the rope box so you could use it if you had to. But if the rope broke and you didn't have a spare, you knotted it at first, and that night you cut the knot out and spliced it to make a nice tidy job. Some boatmen ended up with many splices, but they were all neat enough to work through a pulley block.

Some of the horses were difficult to handle. I was standing by a horse holding on to his tackle waiting for the line to be attached when he suddenly decided to be off. I didn't let go and I was towed up the tow-path on my stomach until eventually he stopped, leaving me all bruised and scratched. Another time, we had just left Stourport with a Belgian mare called Dolly when she started kicking and rearing. I couldn't control her, and she turned round and shot back to Stourport taking the boat line with her. These were exceptions

Horse and longboat at Gas Street Basin in Birmingham

though – most of the horses worked hard and did what was needed
without much telling.

Usually somebody had to walk with the horse. If you didn't have
someone nudging him along a bit, he might walk slowly and let the rope
fall in the canal so you couldn't steer properly. Also, there was a risk
he'd stop and graze if he saw a nice bit of grass, and you couldn't get
ashore easily. You could shout and shout, but you were out in the
middle of the cut! To get off the boat, you had to put your shaft in the
water and leap across, but by then he'd realize what you were up to and
he'd go on again!

If there was just the boatman and his wife, they took it in turns to
walk with the horse, but when you first started as a boy, you usually did
the driving. You walked behind the horse on the hedge side of the rope,
holding on near to where it was attached to the horse's tackle. You
didn't walk on the canal side because if the horse made a sudden turn,
he could chuck you in the canal. The reins were tied on to the tackle and
were only needed very occasionally. Most of the horses kept on walking
if they heard your feet scuffing along behind, and they stopped if you
just asked them. Sometimes you carried a stick, but it was very seldom.

You knew whether your horse needed anything like that. You generally had good animals, and you just shook the spreader and said 'Go on' a bit sternly. You knew you had to rely on that animal so you treated him well and made sure he didn't go without his food.

The horses were like human beings. If the skipper made you drive one too hard because he wanted to keep ahead of a boat that was coming behind, the horse might just stop. One particular horse, Betsy, thought she wouldn't pull any more, and she walked into the canal. She stood there until the boat came alongside, and then the skipper got the shaft and knocked her to get her back on to the tow-path. But as soon as she got her feet back on to dry land, she whipped around and started for home at full gallop. No rope would have held her, and the line broke with the crack of a whip. I had to walk 2 miles back to Worcester stable to fetch her, and it didn't finish there. The stableman wanted to know why that horse came back on her own – had I been beating her. Having walked for 2 miles, I'd no wind for explanations, and he blamed me when really the skipper was more to blame.

When it was a meal time, the skipper had his food out on top of the cabin while he was steering, and then he went ashore and let you go on the boat to have something. Or he might chuck you an old shoe on a length of rope, and you put a couple of stones into the shoe and tied it on the back of the horse. You hit the horse once and dropped the shoe down so that it was making a noise as though you were scuffing along behind. Then when you came to a bridge, you jumped on the boat and ate a bit of bread and cheese before getting off at the next bridge. The horse would keep going, but only for so long, as he soon got to know that it was only an old boot behind him and not the driver!

Some of the skippers were not so thoughtful, and they got drunk and spent all the money so there wasn't any bread in the cupboard. Many a time I've had to get myself a swede out of a field to have something to eat. The lock-keeper's allotments often suffered too. If you were working a bit late at night and you could tell the lock-keeper was asleep, you might go and dig up a couple of carrots or some potatoes and then smooth the soil over afterwards. With some skippers, you had to be a little bit of a thief or you'd starve. I was with one chap who boozed and gambled all the money, and as it was getting dark, he told me to go into a field and get a cabbage. I thought I'd better get a big one, and I struggled with it up to the boat. He brought the stern in towards the tow-path and grabbed the cabbage, but when I got on board at the next bridge, he hit me for six – I had brought back a cow cabbage meant for animals to eat!

You could walk miles and miles with the horse, and sometimes you had to keep going all night as well. One night, I was so tired that my eyes kept closing. I thought to myself that the skipper was so far behind, he wouldn't be able to see me in the dark, so I got on the back of the horse for a ride. Now those boat horses were that clever, it was as though they'd been to school. We came to a low bridge, and as he went under the arch, he rubbed his ribs right against the brickwork and this lobbed me off. I couldn't get off the side he was rubbing, and as I got off the other side, he side-stepped and pushed me into the canal. The skipper heard the splash and shouted out 'What's be going on then?' I had to say I'd been walking on the wrong side of the horse and I'd slipped off the tow-path. 'You ain't got no more sense than you was born with! That horse has got more sense than thee!' Of course I had to put up with all this – the horse was clever, there's no mistake about it.

Some horses would go on walking all day without anyone going near them, and this was known as baccering. You had to watch out for horses coming the other way, but on the Worcester and Birmingham Canal, you knew when to expect them. Going up, they were controlled by the times of the river tugs, and coming down, they were controlled by the times of the tunnel tugs. When you met the first one, you asked how many more were following. You walked with the horse until they had all passed, and then you could start baccering again. You also had to watch out at turnover bridges where the tow-path changed sides, as there was sometimes a choice of routes. After going over the bridge, the horse should turn back towards the boat and then go under the bridge, but if he just carried on, you were in trouble! So usually somebody would jump ashore approaching the bridge and see him round it.

You always carried a whip on the boat, but very seldom did you take it ashore. The steerer might use it if he was to call out 'Gee up', but he didn't hit the horse. The sound was enough to remind the horse to get cracking – he knew what it was all about. On the end of the whip, you tied a silk thrum with three knots in it, so that when you cracked the whip, it sounded like a gun going off. As it wore down to each knot, it fuzzed out, and when the last knot went, you needed another thrum.

To feed the horse, you gave him a nose can of corn as he was going along. In the old days, they put the corn in a basket, and some boatmen still called it this even though it was made of tin. The can was held by a strap over the horses head. You set it up so the corn was just up to his mouth, and later you pulled it up a bit more so he could still reach. You wouldn't drive him hard like that because if he was pulling all the time,

A boat horse with a nose can on the Staffordshire and Worcestershire Canal

he was breathing heavily and getting a flurry of oats up his nose. Then he'd blow his nose to get that down, and he'd blow all his food out of the nose can. So you gave him the can when you came to several locks together, and you let him go on nice and steady between locks. When he'd finished his corn, you took his nose can off, dipped it in the canal and give him a can of water. So he could drink it easily, you stood in front of him with one foot forward, resting the can on your knee. If you left it on the ground, he'd have to drink up his throat and he'd be swallowing against his collar. Some horses could manage that, but others coughed most of it out. When he'd had his drink, he was all right to go on for the next few miles.

Climbing up to Stoke Prior, the horse wouldn't drink the canal water because the salt works made the water salty all the way down to the River Severn. So at Jack Wareing's lock just below the Five Mile Pound, there was a square brick-built tank on the side of the tow-path, and this was filled with water by pumping from a brook down below. The horse could have a drink out of there, and then he wouldn't have any more until he got up past the salt works. Here the horse didn't need telling what to do – once he'd pulled the boat into the lock, he turned round and came back on his own because he knew he was going to get a drink. You'd draw the paddles, and then you gave him a couple of cans of water from the canal which was clear again there.

Going up a flight of locks, a skipper and his mate worked together as a team, using their experience and strength to get their boat through the locks as quickly as possible. Approaching the first lock, the driver of the horse ran ahead to get it ready. He carried a windlass to work the paddles tucked into the back of his belt in the form of a 'V'. If the lock was full of water, he would close the single top gate, drop the top paddles and then draw the bottom paddles. He would usually let the paddles drop with a crash and draw them very fast – the only time he worked quietly was if there was a boat in front when he stopped for the night and he was trying to get away first. When the lock was empty, he opened the two bottom gates by standing on the near-side gate and pushing the off-side gate open with his foot and then walking back to push on the balance beam of the near-side gate.

As the horse reached the lock, the driver dropped the near-side paddle and lifted the line over the top of the gate. When the boat was well into the lock, the driver shouted to the horse to stop pulling, drew the off-side top paddle and hurried back to draw the near-side paddle so that the water entering the lock would slow the boat. The boat was also pushing water into the lock, and the bow first dipped into the water and then rose upward. If all went well, the boat was brought to a halt just before it hit the top sill, but every boat had a good fender on the stem just in case. Meanwhile, the steerer had pulled the tiller out of the helm and stood it in the hatchway where he also set up a gate-shutter shaft ready for use later. As the boat entered the lock, he jumped off, ran up the steps, dropped the off-side paddle, and grabbed the gate-shutter. Then he started to close the bottom gates by pushing with the gate-shutter against one balance beam and shoving with his back on the other beam. As the gates began to close, the water pouring through the upper paddle holes and rushing past the boat forced the gates to close with a thud.

While the lock was filling, the driver went ahead to prepare the next lock, and the steerer checked the rudder was not jammed between the gates, stowed the gate-shutter in the hatchway and arranged the line ready for leaving the lock. To start a boat moving is a heavy load for a horse, and so a special arrangement was used to ease the task. The line from the horse was passed through a pulley block fixed to the mast, and a loop on the end was put over a hook fixed in the wing wall of the lock by the corner of the overflow weir. When the lock was nearly full, the steerer shouted to the horse to start pulling, and as the boat moved forward, the top gate was forced open with the steerer also pushing on the balance beam. Once the gate was fully open, the steerer jumped back on board and began steering again. The action of the pulley block continued to ease the load for the horse until a wooden peg in the line reached the block. Then as the horse took up the full load, the boat carried on forward and the loop at the end of the line naturally fell clear of the hook on the wall. All these activities were repeated again and again until the boat had passed through all the locks in the flight. It was usual to leave the top gates open, and then after the last boat in the evening, the lock-keeper came along and shut them so that if any bottom gates were leaking, there wouldn't be too much wastage.

When I first started as a boy, I had a job to work the paddles, so I got on and steered the boat while the skipper went ahead to get the lock ready. As the boat was approaching the lock, he called out 'Towards the chimney a bit' or 'Towards the side bed.' No port or starboard! He knew very well I knew where the side bed was and where the chimney was, and I moved the tiller across as he wanted. When the horse had pulled the boat right up into the lock, the skipper came back and closed the inside gate. I learned to jump off into the steps to pull the other gate to, and he worked the paddles until I was man enough to do it myself.

A wooden boat had to go into a lock dead straight or it would hit the

Horse boat *Frampton* on the Worcester and Birmingham Canal

iron-work at the entrance and you could start the oakum coming out of the seams. If a skipper found his boat was leaking, the foreman usually sent him down to Hempsted dry dock for caulking, and while the boat was there, the skipper didn't get any pay, so it was important to keep the boat in good order. If you made a mistake going into a lock, the skipper would be furious, so the quicker you could jump off up the steps and get away from him the better. One time I was chased halfway up the Thirty, but I was faster than him! His anger didn't last long because he couldn't do without me, but it meant I only had one round of bread that evening instead of two. Severn and Canal boats had a blue flash at the front with a white line round. When a boat hit the iron guard at the mouth of a lock, it made a black mark on that white line (and it was a black mark to the steerer!). If the other boatmen saw the mark, they'd call out 'When are you going to get a new pair of glasses.' So if you made a mistake like that, you got a small tin of white paint and touched it up yourself.

It seemed that some boatmen thought more of their boat than they did of their crew. One poor woman made a mistake steering into a lock, and the skipper threw a brick at her. He'd just drawn a lock off, and the water in the pound hadn't settled down. She got the boat straight for the lock, but then it veered off a bit. He could see what he wanted so he shouted for her to hold in (towards the tow-path), but then the water brought her back and so he shouted to hold out. The poor woman was on the tiller doing what she could to keep the boat from running about, but she wanted some strength to get the tiller across on a loaded boat, and she ended up hitting the lock wall. When the skipper threw the brick at her, he hit the chimney for six, and then he blamed her for that!

While working the locks, the horse was an important part of the team, and a good horse knew what to do with little instruction. As the boat entered the lock, most knew when to stop pulling, and they came back a bit to provide enough slack to run out the block rope. A new horse sometimes kept on pulling until the boat hit the gate, and then you had to go and fetch him back to slacken off the rope. Of course you had to be careful going behind some horses. Once I ducked under the line to go and draw a paddle, and the horse kicked me in my diaphragm. It lifted me back a good 6 ft and knocked the wind out of me. I was carrying a shaft, but I never got it near the horse – he knew he'd done wrong and he bolted off pulling the boat into the top sill! Another time, the horse started grazing while the driver went to get the next lock ready. The steerer went forward with the shaft and splashed in the water, but the

A Severn and Canal horse boat on the Worcester and Birmingham Canal

old horse just looked round and went on munching. Then the steerer set the night afire with his language, and the horse had a muzzle on for the next lock! It was a regular thing to carry a muzzle, although not many needed it.

Going down a lock, the driver of the horse ensured that the top near-side paddle was down, and he lifted the line up over the paddle and the gate. As the boat entered the lock, the steerer held the tiller against his chest, leaving his hands free for a strap which he dropped over the dolly [post] on the top of the gate. He took a turn round the stud on the boat, easing away gently so as not to jerk the strap and break it, and the motion of the boat helped to close the gate. At the same time, the driver opened the bottom near-side paddle, and the water flowing through the lock made the top gate close with a thud.

One time, I didn't lift the line over the top paddle, and I couldn't stop the horse. As the boat came into the lock, the line caught round the ironwork and broke. I didn't see dad coming up behind me with the broken end, and I had it across my backside. That was up at the Engine Lock, and I still had the mark when I got to Worcester at 7 o'clock that night. A boatman was supposed to buy his own straps, but a lot of them used to try to save a few bob by cutting a piece off the farling provided by the company, and this used to get shorter and shorter. The action of the strap pulled the boat against the side of the lock, so many of the boatmen hung a piece of rope over the side of the boat near the fore-end of the cabin to act as a fender.

Once the boat was in the lock, the driver went ahead to prepare the next lock, and the steerer jumped off, released the catch to drop the top off-side paddle and went down to draw the bottom off-side paddle. While the lock was emptying, the steerer placed the line between the 'V' of the bottom gates ready for when they opened. When the lock was empty, the steerer opened the bottom gates, stepping across from one to the other on the footboard, and as the horse started to move the boat forward, the steerer jumped down on to the cabin. When it was icy, it was better not to risk stepping across on the footboards, and instead the steerer could use the gate-shutter shaft to push open the off-side gate.

A difficulty on the Staffordshire and Worcestershire Canal was that there were bridges near some of the locks that the horse couldn't get under. Going up, the horse went past the bridge and kept pulling as far as he could. Then the driver unpegged the line, ran back with the end and dropped it down to the steerer. When the boat had drifted through the bridge, the steerer threw the line back up, and the horse finished pulling the boat into the lock. Going down empty, the horse started the boat out of the lock, and then the driver pulled the eye of the rope off the luby, nipped round the other side of the bridge and put it back on again. The driver could do it himself downhill, but he couldn't do this going up because he'd be using the block and tackle which was lashed on to the mast.

Going along the canal, it was usual to let an empty boat overtake even though it meant that all the locks would be against you. You could stop him by zig-zagging across the canal as your heavy boat could push the empty one where you liked. But it was best to let him go through and get out of your way so you could carry on steadily. If he was a pal of yours, he might repay you by shutting the gates as he went out of the locks, so that all you had to do was to go up and draw the paddles. The loaded boat stayed in the middle of the canal where the water was deepest, and the empty boat came past on the outside where there was more water than on the tow-path side. With all the horses going along the tow-path, it had broken away year by year so that the canal was silted up and weeds were growing on that side. The rope from the empty boat had to go over the top of the loaded boat. As the empty boat stood well above the loaded one, the driver of the horse could easily flip

The horse is waiting on the tow-path opposite Cadbury's warehouse at Bournville until his boat is ready to leave

the rope over the chimney and over the mast, and then he lifted it over the other horse and he was past.

When meeting a boat coming the opposite way, the proper thing was for one horse to stop and let the line go into the bottom of the canal so the other boat could go over the top. But if both skippers wanted to keep going, one line could be lifted over the other horse and boat, particularly if an empty boat was going by on the outside. So when the two horses were approaching one another, one driver would shout out 'Be you going to have it up or under?' If your line was going up, the first thing was to lift the line over the other horse. He knew what was happening, and as you lifted your line, he might lower his head. Once over the horse, your line ran along the other line, and when it came to the luby, you just gave a little flick which travelled along your line and took it over the top. Then the other steerer watched your line coming towards him, and if necessary he lifted it over his chimney and himself and it was clear.

This up and under business didn't always work. If the line got caught on the luby, the other horse had to stop, allowing the luby to bend and throw the line off. But I remember one time the line got caught and the other horse still kept going until eventually he was brought up standing. Only then did the luby bend back and release the line which swept along the planks and caught the steerer round the shoulders. This frightened him to death as he thought he was going to be pulled into the canal. He was able to throw the line clear, but he was so annoyed, he used his shaft to vault off the cabin on to the tow-path and he started taking his jacket off. The driver of the horse managed to calm him down, but there was plenty of bad language!

There were some places where a bridge was on a bend, and you couldn't see if a boat was coming towards you. When you were so far from it, you ran ahead of the horse to have a look. If there was nothing coming, you just stood there, and the old horse would keep on coming at his rate. You didn't go back to the horse, because if he thought you were going back to give him a hiding, he might turn round and go off home! You didn't want that to happen, so you stayed put and called out a little bit of encouragement – 'Come on me old beauty, come on then.'

On the Staffordshire and Worcestershire Canal, there were shallow parts where boats often ran aground. Some coming down with coal or stone had no more sense than to chuck part of their load over the side and that made it worse. If you ran aground, it caused no end of trouble and you lost that much time. The horse couldn't start the boat with a dead pull if it was on the bottom, so you had to put the pulley block on the mast that you used at every lock. Someone had to pole-jump on to the bank on the outside of the canal, run another line up to almost opposite the horse and make it fast to a tree trunk or something. Then with the rope running through the pulley, the horse would find it easier to start, and once he could feel the boat was moving, he'd go like mad to scrape it over that bad place.

During the winter, ice could slow you down and sometimes stop you altogether. The ice got trapped behind the lock gates so you couldn't open them enough for the boat to pass through, and you had to drag the ice out with a boat hook. This could become a job at every lock, and it slowed you down – it was terrible. Also you couldn't risk stepping across the bottom gates, and so you had to walk round and cross over the top gate. One time we were coming down the Thirty below Tardebigge, and it froze that hard we couldn't come any further. They tried to bring an ice boat up the canal from Stoke Prior to release us and the other boats with us. It was an iron boat with two masts and an iron bar between them. They got the boatmen and some of the Canal Company's men standing each side of the bar, and they had six horses pulling while the men rocked the boat to break the ice. When they got stuck, they brought the boat back and started the horses going again. But the ice became so strong that the horses pulled the boat up on the ice and it just skidded along. We took the horses down to the lock above Stoke Prior, and Severn and Canal sent some corn up on a lorry to share out. But we had no help looking after ourselves, and we were stuck there for six weeks. Luckily there happened to be a house nearby that had a well where we could get fresh water. The boatmen that were stuck further up had to walk back up to the lock-keeper's house to get water there. For food, we had to walk up the canal to the road and then into Bromsgrove and back which was five miles. The only money we had was from a farmer who gave us eight shillings a day for hedge cutting and other odd jobs.

For most tunnels, the horse was taken over the top, but for Netherton Tunnel there is a tow-path on either side with railings and the horse had to walk right through. Most boats put a hurricane lamp on the bow to help the horse see where he was going but, to save money, some boatmen made a lamp out of a Brasso tin using a knotted piece of cotton line as a wick. You had to keep into the side to avoid boats coming the other way, and so you used a short line from the mast and let the boat rub along the coping stones of the tow-path all the way. The horse was just about level with the foredeck, and you sat on the deck beside him to keep him going. You daren't let the horse slow down or the boat could come past him and pull him over the railing into the canal, so if he started to ease up, you shook his tackle to encourage him. Often you saw a flickering light coming the other way, and that was an open coal boat which had a fire lit in a tin instead of a stove.

# CHAPTER 5

# *Cargoes and Destinations*

*Severn and Canal Carrying Company longboats carried all kinds of goods through to works and warehouses in Birmingham and the Black Country, and occasionally there were return cargoes to bring back to Gloucester.*

The weight of your cargo was checked at various places to determine what toll had to be paid. Often they relied on what was written on your consignment note, but around Birmingham there were several gauging stops where they measured what inches of freeboard you had. There were four steel gauging plates on the gunnels of the boat – by the mast beam and by the stern beam on either side. When a boat was new, on your first trip up to Birmingham, you had to go to the weighbridge at Smethwick or Tipton. There, they first measured from the plates down to the water level when the boat was empty, and then they kept putting in one ton weights and measuring her all round again and again until she was fully loaded. They put all the measurements on a sheet, and they made this out many times so that all the toll houses could have a copy. At the same time, they gave you a gauging number. Then to check your load at a gauging stop, the man had a stick which was marked in inches. He measured from the gauging plates down to the water level, and then he looked up your sheet to find how much cargo you were carrying. In this way, he could tell your load to the nearest 5 cwt.

The most common place to go was the Severn and Canal warehouse at Bridge Street beside Gas Street Basin in Birmingham. The warehouse had a floor area of 50,000 sq ft on two stories where bulk supplies could be stored, and then small quantities were delivered by road as required by the traders. Much of what we took there was what was called general

*Lenchford* at the Severn and Canal warehouse at Gas Street Basin

cargoes such as cement, paper, tinned foods, confectionery, sugar, soda, soap, etc. We also carried metals such as copper and spelter, and we took carbide for use by the British Oxygen Company. Various sorts of glassware came from the Continent for lighting manufacturers, and we had baths from Germany and fencing from Belgium. You name it – we carried it! At one time Typhoo tea was unloaded there, but in the thirties they had a new factory built beside the canal at Fazeley Street and we took it there.

You often had to wait a couple of days to unload at Gas Street, and you'd join a gang of boatmen unloading the boats before you. There were only four men in the warehouse, and all the rest were boat people – you got a shilling an hour on daywork. When you were called upon, you shafted your boat over to the warehouse, and you had to go to the right berth for what you were carrying. Along the front was the big ton crane for unloading the heavy stuff, and there was room for two boats up the arm where we took tinned milk, tea and sweets etc. Sometimes a case of tea or tinned food would be 'damaged' in handling – we had ways and means of getting everything as free as we could! For heavy stuff, you had to move the boat along to keep under the crane, and instead of untying and re-tying both ends of your boat, you used the ½-cwt log. This was a 56-lb weight on the end of a bit of rope tied to a ring on the side of the quay with the weight hanging over the outside of the boat. When you'd discharged one part of the cargo, you pushed the log along and the boat moved the other way until it was in the right place for discharging the next section. While unloading, the side cloths were rolled down on to the gunnels, and a metal cover was fitted over them to avoid damage.

In the 1920s, Severn and Canal carried considerable quantities of wheat from the ports to mills in the Midlands. Some of it was trans-shipped from the barges at Gloucester, but the longboats also loaded at Sharpness from the pneumatic elevators, *Leitrim* and *Dunkirk*, or from one of the warehouses. The customers included Watson Todd and Co. (Midland Flour Mills, Birmingham), Walter Brown and Sons (Central City Flour Mills, Birmingham), Smith Brothers (Albion Flour Mills, Walsall), Millers of Wolverhampton and Goodwins of Kidderminster. Not all the cargoes of wheat were delivered in full. On the way up the river, you could get underneath the cloths, take some wheat out of each bag and tip it into an empty one. You took less than a bucketful from each so that you could tie the bag up almost the same as it was before. Then there were certain places up the canal where you went to ask if they wanted some wheat. They could have a whole bag for about twenty-five eggs and a pound note. That used to give us a banquet, and we even had boiled eggs for breakfast!

Watson Todd had one of the biggest mills a short way along the Main Line of the Birmingham Canal. Initially, you left the boat at the Bar Lock and walked round to their mill to find out when they wanted to start unloading. Whatever time they said, you had to be there or you missed your turn. You tied the horse on the canal bank and got the boat in under the mill. We called it Todds Hole because they had an arm off the canal approached through an arch, and it was dark inside. You had to put your fire out before you got there or else you'd be choked by the fumes. So far underneath, there was a trap-door in the roof, and the chain on the hoist came down and lifted the sacks up into the mill. Once you were in there, you didn't come out until the last sack was unloaded, and it used to get on my nerves. You could hear the traffic rumbling over the top, and I was afraid that the bricks might start to fall in and bury us.

Going to Smiths Mill at Walsall, you had 300 bags of wheat on board leaving Gloucester, but you couldn't take all that up the Staffordshire and Worcestershire Canal because you'd be too deep. So you had to stop at Stourport, go over to the Long Warehouse and get twenty-five or thirty bags off to lighten the boat. After half a dozen boats had done this, the bags were loaded on to another boat to finish their journey. Smiths also had a warehouse at the Pleck before you got to the mill, and sometimes you delivered part or all of your load there. The mill itself was two locks up from the Walsall level, and when you got there, you had to get your own horse to pull each sack out one at a time using a block and tackle.

All the coal for the mill was piled up on their wharf, and sometimes we took some for our own use. You had to find your own coal, wood, paraffin and everything, and this was the best place for coal. You got the ropes out of the foredeck, half filled it up with coal and then coiled the ropes down on top in case somebody looked inside. To try to stop this pilfering, the mill people began to whitewash the coal so they could see if any had been taken. But they didn't reckon on the brains of the boatmen, and when we went there next time, we took our own whitewash! After dark, we had about 5 or 6 cwt, and then we smoothed over what was left and whitewashed it. Next morning the mill foreman came looking at the coal, and he couldn't see anything wrong as it was all white with no breaks in it!

When taking wheat to Goodwins Mill at Kidderminster, you went through Kidderminster Lock, and on the left was a swing-about crane with a big wheel. You started winding and then let go, so it pulled the bag up so far and then you caught the handle and carried on. You had to use your boat horse to go and fetch a hopper truck which ran on rails through the property of a carpet factory to a point just below the tow-path. The hopper was square at the top and tapered down to a square hole with a steel plate across it. You put a plank across the hopper, lowered each bag on to it, untied the string, tipped the wheat into the hopper and put the empty sack back into the boat. You emptied the sacks into the hopper until it was nearly full, and then the boat horse pulled it along towards the mill.

Severn and Canal longboats picked up timber direct from ships at Sharpness. To get it into the boat, you had to take out all the beams except the middle one. You had to leave that in place or the sides of the boat would be pushed in and the oakum could come out of the seams. The other beams were not so important because the dockers packed the timber in tight up to the sides of the boat – they had an art to their work. You could only get about 23 tons into a boat, because if you put in any more it was a top heavy job. A regular place we took timber to was

*Linnet* at Kidderminster

Williams and Farmer's yard next to the Severn and Canal Warehouse at Gas Street Basin. One time the men there refused to unload a boat as they'd been two days on the dole and they had to get three days together to claim any money. So the boatman and and his ten-year-old grandson had to unload and stack the timber, and it took them all day. We also took timber to Coventry. I can always remember that, because as boys we were all crazy to go and see Lady Godiva. We thought we were going to see something sparkling, and when we got there, she was only a statue!

In the early 1920s, tons and tons of timber were taken to Blackpole near Worcester for building Cadbury's factory there. To make the boats carry more up the river, they tied them together in pairs with big fenders between and loaded them up like a lighter. Once the wood was at cabin level, they started putting planks across both boats, and then they put alternate layers criss-crossed until they had two boat loads on the top. The timber was built up over the cabins, and they made a stage for the steerer to stand on so he could see ahead. You turned the tillers over so they were cocked up, and you had a rope across between the tillers and another rope tying the rudders together. Then if you pulled one tiller over, the other would follow, and the two rudders acted as one. The timber was also built up over the foredeck, but you could stoop underneath to put the tow rope on the timberhead. Then you could take the boats up the river like that with no trouble, and you only needed one steerer for the two boats. Nothing could turn them over, and they were easy to tow because the water went down between them and didn't build up at the front.

Each pair of longboats was taken into the basin just above Diglis Lock at Worcester, and empty longboats were brought alongside. All the boatmen had to help take off the top layers, handling one or two pieces of wood at a time. As each boat was loaded, away he went to Blackpole, and when all the top layers were removed, the linked boats were separated and also went up the canal. At Blackpole, there was a crane that could lift out five or ten pieces at a time and put them on a flat bogie. This ran on a line for about a quarter of a mile along the canal bank where the timber was stacked up. But the men there used to take their time, and it could be very slow unloading. You couldn't touch it because it was their job to discharge – not yours. When it was busy, our people could fill the boats at Diglis as fast as they could get empty ones down, and at one time boats were queuing from the top of the Four [locks] up to Blackpole waiting to discharge.

Transferring timber from lighter to longboat at Worcester

Even when the factory was completed, we still carried on taking timber to Blackpole for use in making boxes. Coming down empty from Birmingham, sometimes they stopped you at Worcester and gave you orders to load timber from a lighter in the basin off the river. You took as much as you could without making the load top heavy. You didn't worry about the delay in getting back to Gloucester – it was better to be earning money. In the evening, you could always go into Worcester for the cinema. If you were moored at Blackpole, you walked that 4 miles to go to the pictures, and then you walked back along the tow-path afterwards eating fish and chips from a newspaper.

Severn and Canal did a lot of carrying to the Cadbury's factories at Bournville and Blackpole on the Worcester and Birmingham Canal and Frampton on the Gloucester and Sharpness Canal. In the early days, Cadbury's had their own boats doing this work, but they had so much business, they also had to use Severn and Canal boats to keep up with the orders. In the 1920s, there were sure to be three or four boats going to Bournville every week. They had a warehouse beside the canal with an overhanging canopy, and they had three cranes – one for cocoa beans, one for crumb and sugar and one for other stuff. Even if all the boats had the same cargo, you had to unload at the one crane, and you had to wait your turn to use that berth. At Bournville, the cocoa beans were crushed and moulded to make big square cakes of what was called chocolate mass. Four or five blocks in a sack weighed about 1 cwt, and we brought that back to Frampton. There the mass was cut up and mixed with sugar and condensed milk to make a raw form of chocolate known as crumb which we took back to Bournville for final processing.

The sugar usually came into Gloucester on steamers of the Bristol Steam Navigation Company and the Standard Line, and it was loaded direct overside into longboats. Sometimes the sugar came to Gloucester in railway trucks instead, and it was transferred to the longboats in front of Severn and Canal's warehouse using casual labour made up from waiting boat crews. The sugar was in bags weighing almost 2 cwt. Two men were put up in the first truck to get the bags up-ended on the edge of the truck, and two men carried the bags to the longboat on their shoulders. You put the first three bags down on the quayside one on top of the other. Then you dropped the other bags on top, slid them down on to the side of the boat and the skipper stowed them. As you discharged each truck, they moved the longboat along to the next truck. They used to have bags that were tied too tightly, and when you

Loading a longboat with sugar beside the Western Wall (Llanthony Quay), Gloucester

dropped them down, some would split up the side and away would go the sugar. So they changed to bigger bags that were loosely tied, and they just flopped down and didn't burst. These bags wrapped round your neck like a scarf, and without protection your neck used to bleed by the time you'd finished. But most men had a red kerchief with white spots, and they wrapped this round their neck to stop getting sore.

When you had discharged sugar at Frampton, if they didn't want you to load crumb, you came back to Gloucester and you were first turn again, but after a second trip to Frampton, you were last turn after any boats already in the docks. Your turn depended on whether you came through Llanthony Bridge before or after boats from the river came out of Gloucester Lock. This sometimes led to arguments, and it was no use appealing to the bridge-keeper or anyone. You had to settle it between yourselves before the foreman gave out the next orders, and occasionally the arguments became heated and punches were thrown.

In the thirties, Severn and Canal chartered ships to bring 500-ton cargoes of sugar into Sharpness or Bristol for Cadbury's, and they brought it to Gloucester in barges, transferred it into boats and used the boats as warehouses. Some boats could lie there for weeks as they could only deal with two or three a day at Frampton, and this was very unpopular with the boatmen as it wasn't until they had discharged that they could take their turn for a load of chocolate back to Bournville. If you wanted some sugar, you pushed a piece of copper pipe in through the mesh of the sack, and the sugar ran out. You could have 10 lb or so, and when you pulled the pipe out, the hole closed up behind. They knew we used to have it, but they never checked the weight.

The milk came from local farms, and at one time Cadbury's had their own boats' collecting churns left at the bridges along the Gloucester and Sharpness Canal. At Frampton, the milk was condensed, and the chocolate mass and sugar were blended in to form a thick gluey mess which was tipped out into big trays and heated in an oven. When it had been cooked so long, the raw chocolate came out as slabs which were crushed to give little lumps of chocolate crumb, and this was stored in a big hopper and then put into bags. When the crumb was fresh made, it was so hot you had a job to hold the bags in your hands as you were loading them. Each bag weighed 1 cwt, but they varied in size, as those with only large lumps were much bigger than those containing a lot of dust. The usual load was 460 bags weighing 23 tons. If you had a lot of big bags, the boat could be too top heavy, so you tried to get as many small ones as you could. They were not weighed at the other end, so if you wanted some crumb to eat, you could easily take a few pounds out of a big bag and they'd never know.

When you arrived at Frampton to load crumb, the foreman came and checked your canvas, and if it had a smell, he sent you back to Gloucester. The canvas cloths were waterproofed once a year using a green stuff called pey. Severn and Canal cloths were always black and shiny, and they reckoned that this was because they put half a bucket of fish oil mixed in with the pey. Sometimes this fish oil might smell, so you had to wait 6 to 8 weeks before loading cargoes like sugar or chocolate crumb. If the foreman couldn't smell anything that might get to the sacks of crumb, you were all right to load, but if you had some bulky sacks, you had to lay empty ones on top to keep the cloths away from the crumb.

Usually we took the crumb to Cadbury's main factory at Bournville, but sometimes it went to Blackpole for storage there and then on by road to Bournville when they needed it. Another cargo for Blackpole was ½-cwt bales of strawboard that came up on our barges to Gloucester. This was like cardboard, and it was used for making boxes and cartons for

Unloading sacks of sugar at Cadbury's warehouse at Bournville

putting the chocolates in. At Cadbury's places particularly, you were often held up waiting to unload, and then there was a mad rush to get you away before you came on to demurrage. If they couldn't empty you in forty-eight hours, you got 5s a day and the company got 9s – even if you were only a few minutes over. The time started from when you got your consignment note into the office, so you always tried to get there before they closed at 5 o'clock or otherwise you couldn't put it in until 7 o'clock next morning. When approaching Blackpole, you often ran ahead of the boat to get the note in while the horse was still coming up the pound. This was particularly important on a Friday because if you were late, you couldn't clock in until Monday. But they did anything to stop you getting that demurrage. I reckon they paid the blokes a bonus, because they used to work very hard to get you away, and if you slowed them down, they shouted for you to go faster. I had a load of bags pulled out in an hour and forty minutes, and the foreman laughed at us, saying 'I've done you!'

We took spelter to Stewarts and Lloyds at Halesowen, and where we discharged was a big high wall with a crane that was higher than a house. To get there, we went through a narrow tunnel [Gosty Hill 577 yd]. During the day, boats were taken through by a tug which had a propeller at each end. There were that many boats waiting, it couldn't turn round, so they just locked the tiller at one end and reversed the engine to push them back again. The tug finished at 5 o'clock, so if you wanted to start home after that, you had to leg through. As the tunnel was only just about as wide as the boat, you had to be careful as you went in that there was nobody coming the opposite way, but as it was mainly used by day boats carrying coal which tied up when the tug finished, you were usually on your own. You laid on your back on top of the cabin and walked along the roof of the tunnel. Someone had to take the horse over the top, so there might be only one person legging and then it took longer, but once you were through the tunnel, you could keep on going.

There were many other places where we used to take cargoes. We took barley and malt up to the vinegar brewery at Stourport and unloaded it there out on the river. The river bank was 30 to 40 ft from the warehouse wall, so when the hoist pulled the sacks out of the boat, they used to drag across the ground and then up a plank. In the 1920s, we fetched tin plate from a works at Wilden Pool on the River Stour by going through a lock from Stour Pound. Later we took steel to a wire mill at the same place. There wasn't room to turn by the works, so you had to drop down with the stream stern first, using lines to the bank, and then you could pull back up again when empty. We took glass sand to a glass works at Stourbridge. They made ornaments there, and the workmen gave us a swan and some cygnets. We took china clay to the Potteries district. It was horrible thick solid mud, and it took you months to get your boat clean afterwards. We took big slabs of glucose in sacks for the brewery at Stratford-upon-Avon. It was very hard, like lumps of rock, and the kids used to keep a bit in their pocket. In those days, we carried everything you could think of.

As soon as you had discharged in the Birmingham area, you went round to the Severn and Canal office in Bridge Street or 'phoned them to see if they had a load for you to bring back. Usually there wasn't anything, and you had to come back empty, but sometimes you were lucky. Occasionally we went out along the Birmingham Canal to fetch things from a foundry that had to come to Gloucester to be shipped abroad, and we picked up slag and took it down to Frampton for the farmers to spread over the fields. Also we went to Stewarts and Lloyds at Halesowen to collect steel tubes, and we went to the Potteries to collect fire-bricks and retorts which were loaded into our barges to go to Bristol.

Sometimes we went down the Thirteen [Farmers Bridge Locks] to Holbrook's vinegar works, and we loaded barrels of vinegar and cases of sauce. You had to make sure each barrel was the right way up with the plug at the top. You often had to wait your turn to go down the Thirteen, and sometimes there were arguments with men from other companies, like Fellows Morton and Clayton. One Gloucester boat was at the top of the Thirteen when another boat came up behind and tried to persuade the Gloucester chap to let him go first. The Gloucester man knew that a boat coming up had made the locks ready, and he got his boat right to the knuckle of the lock so the other bloke couldn't get by even if he tried. Then an argument started, there was some pushing and shoving, and the wives start screaming their heads off. 'If I comes ashore, I'll square him up!' 'You shut your mouth!' 'I'll fix him!' Sometimes these incidents ended in a fight, but I never saw a Gloucester man lose. He'd go in that lock first, whether he'd got a black eye or whatever. Down this way the boatmen had to be tough, carrying sacks of wheat and God knows what. Those Fellows Morton men had it a bit more on the easy side.

The Gloucester men also had to use their ingenuity at times. One of the locks down the Thirteen was a little shorter then the rest, and one of

Longboats moored by Cadbury's warehouse at Bournville

the Severn and Canal boats which was slightly oversize couldn't fit into it when coming up well loaded. Even with the fenders off and the bow right up against the top sill, the crew couldn't quite close the bottom gate. Not wanting to return to discharge their cargo, they filled some empty sugar bags with rubble and laid them along the weir of that pound while the lengthman wasn't looking. Then by drawing paddles, they let water run down the flight to raise the level of the pound until the bow of the boat could protrude over the top sill. This allowed the bottom gate to be closed, and they could carry on back to Gloucester.

Some boats went through the Gullentine [the guillotine lock at the entrance to the Stratford Canal] to collect chalk from Sturge's factory the other side of the next bridge. There was nowhere to turn, so we went in stern first as it's a lot easier going backwards empty than coming backwards fully loaded. The factory was near a heave-up bridge, which was almost balanced and you had to pull it up with your hand. Seven big cylindrical wooden drums, called pipes, filled a longboat, and we had to make sure our canvas came right down to the side of the boat as it was important that the pipes didn't get wet. They were later loaded into

Severn and Canal barges at Gloucester to go to Bristol and on to France where the chalk was used for making into face powder.

Sometimes you picked up a load of salt at Stoke Prior on the way home. The most common type was agricultural salt which was carried loose. You went to one particular bay, and two men brought a big truck carrying about ½ ton and tipped it down a chute into the boat. If you also had to load any special types of salt, you kept this separated from the agricultural salt by a spare section of false flooring or a piece of canvas. There were squares of salt which were tapered blocks weighing about 6 lb, and these went to the shops where they cut chunks off according to how much a customer wanted. There were dairy lumps in 2-lb packets for the kitchens of big houses. Bacon curing salt was in white sacks with a lining to stop the damp going through, and butter salt was specially refined and came in tubs like little half-barrels.

Most of the coal traffic was handled by smaller firms, but Severn and Canal boats sometimes called at Littleton Colliery on the Staffordshire and Worcestershire Canal to bring back coal for the company's tug based at Stourport. You unloaded in the pound between the barge locks, and the coal was tipped down into a former dry dock, from the bottom of which a short tunnel led to the river bank where the tug moored. Occasionally you went to Cannock Chase to get a load of coal for the lock-keepers down the Worcester and Birmingham Canal or the bridgemen on the Sharpness Canal.

Coming down the Staffordshire and Worcestershire Canal, we sometimes picked up a load of sand from a big quarry just below Falling Sands. It was red sand that they used in the foundries for casting, and Sissons was one of the regular customers. We unloaded in the Old Arm or on the North Quay at Gloucester, and they came and collected it by horse and cart. One unusual return cargo from Birmingham was a load of string that was needed urgently in Gloucester, and we agreed to push on all night to bring it down. We also picked up a load of diver's gear that was left for us beside a lock just below the reservoir. It was very heavy to load into the boat in the dark as it included boots, diving suit and copper helmet, but they were so pleased to have all the stuff at Gloucester, we were given first turn to load again.

A very unusual trip was when we were sent from Birmingham to Ellesmere Port to fetch a load of wheat back to Millers of Wolverhampton. We went round through West Bromwich and Oldbury to Wolverhampton, down the locks and on to join the Shropshire Union at Cut End where the stop lock just had a fall of an inch or two. We had a very good mule who kept on going without a driver, and then we met another boat which was also baccering. When the two horses met, the air was blue as the boatman coming the opposite way was cursing and threatening to jump on the bank for a fight. We were in the wrong because we didn't know we should only have been baccering one way on the Shropshire Union – we'd never been that way before. So we let go our cut line and turned into the side, and the other boat managed to pass with no loss of water cans or anything. As our boat was empty, we could jump ashore, recover the line and start the horse going again. After that we kept a look-out for other boats and put someone ashore in good time. If it was too shallow to get in close, we used the shaft to pole-vault on to the bank.

To find the way to Ellesmere Port, we asked the lock-keepers and some of the other boatmen. The boats in that area only carried 18 to 23 tons, and the crews said they wished they had boats like ours as pay depended on the tonnage carried. When we got near Chester, we joined a bigger canal where the locks would take two of our longboats and some were very deep. At Ellesmere Port, we loaded wheat out of a warehouse, and took it back to Millers of Wolverhampton. Having discharged, we went into the office to get our tickets signed, and they gave us a message to go back to Ellesmere Port again to load wheat for Watson Todds. When we got back from that trip, we returned to Gloucester, having done 460 miles.

# CHAPTER 6
# *Owners*

*If a man had his own longboat, he was known as an owner or a bye-trader. In the 1920s, there were owners based in towns and villages down the Severn and along the Stroudwater Canal. Most concentrated on taking hay to the Midlands and coming back with coal or stone. Hay was grown on both sides of the river all the way down from Worcester to Gloucester, and this Severn meadow hay was well thought of in the Midlands as it had more herbage than that from other areas. The coal was brought back to the riverside towns and villages for domestic use. A few of the owners carried more general cargoes and also helped out the Severn and Canal Carrying Company when it was busy.*

One of the principal owners was James Dudfield at the Haw Bridge who handled about 2,000 tons of hay a year. He had 200 acres of meadowland of his own, and he bought from other farmers in Tirley and the surrounding villages. He had two longboats taking hay up to the Midlands and bringing coal back, and he also had two boats going down to Gloucester to put hay on to the railway there. His brother had a farm near the Mythe Bridge, and hay from there was taken by boat to Tewkesbury and put on the railway by Healings Mill.

Dudfield bought hay by the rick, and when it was ready to be dispatched, he sent a gang of trussers to cut it up. One man on the rick used a big two-handled hay knife to cut ½-cwt at a time as near as he could, and another man carried it down and dropped it on the scales for weighing. The scales were made from a pyramid of three poles with a balance pole hanging from the top, and this had a little platform at one end with a ½-cwt weight on and a lazy-back at the other end that they laid the hay on. If the truss weighed a bit too much, the weigher pulled out a handful or two, and if it wasn't quite enough, he added some more. Then each truss was tied up with a band of twisted hay and taken to the boat.

Often the haystacks were on the river bank, and trusses from these were loaded directly into the boats moored right alongside. The farmer bundled the trusses of hay down the bank to the mate standing on the gang-plank, and he carried them on to the boat for the captain to stow. If the rick was away from the river, they hauled the trusses down to the Haw Bridge and covered them up with a tarpaulin until it was convenient to load the boat.

You'd get about seventy trusses in each layer in the boat, and you had five layers making it about 8 ft to the top of the hay. It was piled straight up, slightly narrower than the boat itself, and it had a flat top that you could walk along. After loading four layers, one man put the side cloths up, and the other man used the tiller to hit the sides of the hay to keep it slightly inside the width of the boat. Otherwise, if it was protruding, the side cloth could get ripped on a lock-side. Then you put the final layer on, spread the top cloths over and tied ropes over the top. A boat-load of hay was about 8 or 9 tons – you couldn't carry any more because it would be top heavy and also you wouldn't get under the canal bridges. If it was big green hay, just right, you had about $7\frac{1}{2}$ to 8 tons, but if the hay was a bit close because the rick had got heated, you could have $8\frac{1}{2}$ or 9 tons on.

When the loading was well advanced and you wanted to go away the

Loaded hay boats just above the Haw Bridge

next day, you shouted to the captain of the afternoon tug as he came down, and you asked him to give you a blow as he came up the next day. Then in the morning, he gave you a blast about half a mile before he got to where you were moored, and that gave you time to get ready. If you missed the tug in the afternoon, you had to be prepared in good time for the one in the morning. As soon as the tug captain saw you were intending to hang on to him, he eased down and picked you up as he went by.

As a lightly loaded boat is difficult to steer, a hay boat was always put on a separate short rope close up to the stern of the tug or even alongside it. Just after one Christmas break, when they'd all had a day or two at home, I remember four hay boats going from the Haw Bridge on the same tug. They had two just on the stern quarters of the tug and one each side almost alongside the bow. The hay was always piled up higher than the width of the boat, and the steerer had to stand on the cabin so he could see over the top. You had to be very careful when you went up by the lapper ditches below Wainlode Hill after a flood because the water draining off the fields came sweeping right across the river, especially if the level was dropping down quickly, and one hay boat was turned over there.

Going up the river, you paid a toll at Tewkesbury Lock. The boat was quite a way below the top of the lock, so the lock-keeper had a long stick with a clip on the end which he lowered down to the boat, you put the money in and he gave you a ticket back. He took your word for how much cargo you had, although he could tell within a ton or so just by looking. You paid at Worcester for the tugging and for going on the Worcester and Birmingham Canal – again the lock-keeper took your word for the cargo. Also at Worcester, you hired a horse and you had to go and catch your own from the meadow. Dudfield's boats usually went up the Worcester cut, but a hay boat could be badly affected by wind, and some skippers preferred the Stour cut because it was more sheltered. Also there was a better chance of selling some hay going up the Stour cut.

Once up in the Birmingham area, the captain of the boat sold the hay for the best price he could get. He had a good idea who the likely customers were, and if the first didn't want it, he went somewhere else. He sold the whole boat-load to one customer if he could, but otherwise he sold a bit at a time, and each customer would pay him. Dudfield supplied a lot of hay to Worcester Wharf for the railway horses, to Lavenders at West Bromwich, to Bilston Council at Millfield near the steelworks and to Wolverhampton cattle market. He didn't send much to the collieries as other owners went there. Dudfield also had contracts with Birmingham Corporation for 100 tons at a time, and then there was nothing for the skipper to do as the hay was paid for by cheque.

When the skipper had sold his hay, he took the boat on to a colliery on Cannock Chase. At one time, there were lots of collieries working, and a man stood where the canal branched off and gave the skipper a pound to go to his particular colliery. They also gave 'the long pull' as they called it – a ton or so over what was paid for. By the 1920s, some of those seams were worked out, and we mainly went to Cannock or Littleton collieries. Once we went to Greensforge (Ashwood) Basin to get Baggeridge Wood coal from off Lord Dudley's estate, but it was rotten powdery stuff – you only had to give it a tap and you had nothing but a lot of dust.

Generally they started loading the stern-ruck towards the cabin end, where they put about 14 tons of household coal, and then they often loaded 12 tons of best coal in the fore-end before the mast. In the centre, they put 7 tons of cobbles, which were pieces as big as my fist for use in a range. Some of the chunks of best coal were ½-cwt in weight, and if these had fallen down, it wouldn't have done the bottom of the boat much good. So you put the first pieces down carefully to form a layer that broke the fall of the others. To avoid getting the different types mixed, you built a wall at the end of the best coal, and you built another wall at the end of the household coal before putting the cobbles in between. When the boat was loaded, you put the side cloths up and then the top cloths all the way along. This wasn't necessary for the canal, but if it was a bit rough coming down the river, you could get water blowing over, and without cloths you could have a boat load of water!

Dudfield's coal yard was about a quarter of a mile above the Haw Bridge. You brought the boat as close to the bank as possible, but as she needed about 4 ft of water, you had to set up planks to get the coal ashore. Two men called hobblers worked in the boat. They started breaking down the household coal, using their hands to lift the biggest lumps out, and when they got to the bottom of the boat, they started shovelling. They put the coal into a hand barrow, which was a shallow box with handles at each end, and carried it ashore. When they'd done the household coal, they moved to the fore-end and got the 12 tons of best out, and then they did the nuts in the centre part last.

The captain and his mate had a weighing machine half way between

Using a hand barrow to unload coal at Brimscombe Mills

the boat and the yard. They adjusted the contents of each hand barrow to give the required weight before taking it up into the yard where the coal was stored in $\frac{1}{2}$-ton piles. A hand barrow of big coal, called a draft, was made to weigh $2\frac{1}{4}$ cwt, and you had four of these to the $\frac{1}{2}$-ton. The skipper had a board and a piece of chalk, and he put down three strokes and one across to indicate half a ton. When it came to the cobbles, he had to put extra sides on the hand barrow to stop the cobbles rolling off, but even then it only carried 2 cwt, and so you had five to the $\frac{1}{2}$-ton.

Settling up for the trip didn't take place until the boat was loaded with hay again and ready for the next trip. Then the skipper went to see James Dudfield, taking a list of money spent on tugging, canal tolls, horse hire and perhaps a new cut line. He handed over the money from the hay and collected his share less any advance given to his wife while he was away. Dudfield paid for the coal direct to the colliery.

As well as the two boats going up the river, Dudfield had two more that took hay down to Gloucester to put on the railway there for Birmingham. A lot was sent to Fortnam's at Willenhall and to Atkins' at Darlaston. It wasn't worth sending it all the way by boat as there was no trade to come back with. In the early days, the two boats were usually tied together abreast, and they carried 20 tons of hay with a crew of three. We went down to Gloucester on the tug and took the hay to the

Great Western wharf below Llanthony Bridge. We did send a bit on the Midland Railway from Bakers Quay, but it was more inconvenient. To unload the boats, you caught hold of each truss and threw it up on to the quayside, and a hobbler carried it on his head to a railway truck where the captain of the boat stacked it. When the boats were empty, we brought them back on the tug to where the next load was waiting.

In later years, the trade was less and we only took a single boat to Gloucester. One time we had the boat loaded at Cockbury Hall, just below Chaceley Stock, and down came the tug *Victor* with a tow of boats behind. I gave a rope to a barge they'd picked up from Healings, but they didn't slack up sufficiently, and when I put half a turn round the timberhead, the rope snapped. We were using the old boat, *Betsy*, which had old equipment, and all the good ropes were on the boat that went up country. The tug skipper had to stop the tug and there was a lot of shouting and bawling while he came back to pick us up.

Another time, we were ready to leave the Haw Bridge at 8 o'clock in the evening, and so we decided to drift down. It was a lovely night when we started, but as we got to Wainlode Hill, the fog came down and I could't see where we were. After a time I just caught sight of the cock on top of Ashleworth church above the fog. I knew I ought to get my mate Fred ashore with a line before we got to the Parting, but there were withy bushes overhanging the banks and we couldn't get close in. I was on the fore-end of the boat using the big Severn shaft to try to keep her on the Sandhurst side of the river, but I couldn't feel any bottom – just mud. Eventually I managed to get some leverage against the mud, and the stern of the boat went close enough to the bank for Fred to jump ashore with a line. I thought we'd be all right then, but when we got to the Parting at about 1 o'clock in the morning, we got stuck on the shallow corner where it was all soft mud. I tried to use the shaft to get us off, but I could push it in nearly out of sight before finding a firm bottom, and I had to be careful not to force the boat too far out into the river or we'd be going down towards Maisemore weir. We had a hell of a game fiddling about for an hour in the dark before we got into the Gloucester channel. I wouldn't do that again for all the tea in China!

Of the other owners, most specialized in hay and coal like James Dudfield. The Ball family had 60 acres of meadows at Tirley, and they had one boat. As well as the hay, Tom Ball took cider and apples with him, and he stopped at so many places that he was away for a month at a time, whereas most took only a fortnight. Other hay and coal dealers included Oliver Gaskin at the Haw Bridge and James Young at

James Dudfield's *Dove* near the Haw Bridge

Maisemore. On Gloucester Quay, there were four coal merchants, and they had their own boats which also took hay up. Frank Hipwood had a big yard opposite the old Custom House, and then came William Smith, Majors and J.B. Williams. Also based in Gloucester were William Giddins and Henry Rice, and to the south were Reuben Russell of Quedgeley, Ernest Taylor of Hardwicke, Frank Cookley of Upper Framilode, William Timbrell of Paganhill, Stroud, and James Smart of Chalford. The Stroudwater boats were known as Gothams. In the villages, there was never any difficulty in getting young men to work on the boats as it was a way of seeing the world. In those days, the country people couldn't travel easily, whereas when the boat crews were up in the Midlands, they could go to a football match or even a theatre. The younger fellows heard talk of this in the pub, and their sole idea was to get on the boats.

Charlie Ballinger of Gloucester carried more general cargoes. He took matches to Morelands warehouse by an arm off the Muck Turn at Birmingham, the light boxes being piled right up to the planks the full width of the boat making a square shape under the cloths. He occasionally loaded broken glass jars and bottles, brought to the Quay by horse and cart from Stephens pickle and jam factory, and he took them to a glass works in Birmingham to be used again. Often he went to Tewkesbury to load flour from Healings Mill for Birmingham, and sometimes he carried chocolate crumb to Bournville when Severn and Canal were busy.

Before the First World War, several of the owners based at villages near the Severn had their own horses that they used for towing up the river as well as along the canals, and then they had no tugging to pay. The river tow-path was on the Sandhurst side from Gloucester up to Ashleworth, on the west side to Upton upon Severn and then it crossed back to the Severn Stoke and Kempsey side for the rest of the way to Worcester. Gradually the withy bushes began to get over the river banks making it awkward to tow with a horse, and so a captain took the boat up on the tug while the mate went with the horse all the way to Worcester by road. Then when he met the boat at Worcester, they could carry on without any wait. After the war, it was more usual to hire a horse or a pair of donkeys at Worcester, but sometimes there was none available and you had to wait for a boat to come back down the canal.

The owners who used the Stroudwater Canal mostly had their own pairs of donkeys, and these also towed up the Sharpness Canal until they reached the break in the tow-path at Monk Meadow Dock. Then

Discharging timber from Henry Rice's *Success* at Cadbury's factory at Blackpole

the donkeys were given a gee-up and the tow rope was released so that the boat drifted over to Bakers Quay on the other side of the canal. From there the boat was worked through the docks by bow-hauling and using a hook-shaft. At Gloucester Lock, the two donkeys stepped off a low part of the wall on to the boat ready for going up the river behind the tug. When loading the boat, the owner had left a space in the cargo known as the lay-do, and the donkeys stood there facing up the river all the way to Worcester. They had a nose can of corn to eat, and a bit of canvas was put down in case they made a mess during the day. While rising in the lock up into Worcester basin, they knew to step off the boat, and they walked round to the corner of the basin ready to start off up the canal. During the 1926 General Strike, William Timbrell was tied up in Birmingham, and when he went to the pubs around there, he earned more money or drinks for showing his donkeys than he would have done working his boat!

The owners mostly got their coal from Cannock Chase – that was the best. When you got to the colliery, you booked your turn, but sometimes you had to wait days. There were so many of those Birmingham open boats carrying coal for the big power stations, and their crews left an empty boat in the queue and took the next one that came out loaded, so they were off home. Also it depended what seam the miners were working in. I remember as a boy once having to wait there seven days, and I didn't know where the next bit of bread was coming from. It almost broke me in half wishing I was home, and it made me feel like walking!

If you went up the Worcester canal with a horse you hired from Worcester and you came back down the Stour cut, you had to walk that horse to Worcester and then catch a boat back from Worcester to Stourport to pick up your boat. Sometimes you had to ring for a tug to come up and fetch you because there wasn't a regular service going up to Stourport in the late twenties. If there was no tug, you could drift down the river. You had one fellow on the tow-path with a line attached to the stud just in front of the helm. To start off, he gave a bit of a touch to get the fore-end out in the stream, and then he walked down by the side. If necessary, he could pull the stern in or hold her back to give a bit of steerage way, but once you had a loaded coal boat pointing downstream, it would usually keep going. If you were getting near to a weir, you used the pig – a heavy weight that you dragged behind on a rope to slow you down.

The normal current would be 2 or 3 miles an hour, but if there was a big bank of water in, you might come down at 8 miles an hour. In times of flood, boats were brought down over the weirs – my old grandfather once drifted from Stourport all the way to the Haw Bridge. When they got to Upton, there wasn't enough headroom to get under the bridge, and they needed it to be swung open. Fortunately they met a tug a little way above Upton, so they shouted to the captain to give a blast on the hooter, and the bridge was opened for them to go through. Another boat was drifting down when the river was bank full, and it got stuck across two of the piers of Worcester bridge. The water was brushing up against the side of the boat so much that a fly could have drunk off the gunnel, and they were lucky not to get swamped.

When unloading at one of the coal yards on Gloucester Quay, you had to put up planks between the boat and the steps set into the wall. The boat couldn't go alongside the wall or the planks would be too steep, so she was held out in the river by poles. You pushed a wooden trestle down into the mud just off the quay wall, and you worked it about to get it level. Then you put one plank from the boat to the trestle and another up on to the steps.

The skipper loaded the big coal on to a hand barrow, and then two of us carried it across the planks while the skipper filled another one. When I had to cross the planks for the first time, I was frightened to death and I had to get a grip of myself. I was taught what to do by a good mate who was always waiting on the Quay ready to help for a bit of bread and cheese or whatever the skipper had to give him. He was deaf and dumb, but he'd point and grunt, and you got to know what he meant. You both had to start off with the left foot and keep in step right up to the top. As you were climbing, the plank was going up and down, so you took the first few barrows lightly loaded until you got the rhythm. Then the skipper piled the coal right up making the load about 2 cwt.

For unloading the smaller pieces of coal, we used baskets. When one had been filled by the skipper, you got it on your shoulder, climbed a little ladder inside the boat and walked up the planks. While you were away, the skipper filled another one for your mate to carry. As you lightened the boat, you could pull her closer in to the wall and take one plank away. Three men could discharge 30 tons of coal in just over half a

Frank Cookley's *Bess* with a load of coal

day. Of course some of the coal fell off the barrow into the river, and you couldn't try to stop it or else you'd be in the river too. So when the boat was empty and moved away, the skipper got out the rake that every boat carried, and he raked the coal up into the slipway. Then he put it in a bag and took it home, knowing that if he was stopped, he could just say he'd dragged it out of the river!

During the summer months, instead of bringing coal, some of the boats brought stone for the County Council to put on the roads. We fetched it from a quarry on Rowley Beacon – you went through the Bar Lock, out to Smethwick and then took a branch to the left [Titford Canal]. The stone came down on a railway operated by a cable so that the loaded trucks took the empty ones back up. As each truck came alongside, they dropped the side down and let the stone fall into the boat. When you had twelve tons in the aft-end, you shifted the boat to load 8 tons into the middle, and then you shifted her again to load 7 tons into the fore-end. The stone was discharged on the river bank just above the Haw Bridge. It was put into wheel-barrows and taken ashore across planks, although if the water level was high, the boat could sometimes get in close enough for the stone to be just thrown out on to the bank. From the Haw Bridge, it was taken by horse and cart to various road-side sites to be broken up by gangs of men with hammers.

For overhauls and repairs to their boats, the owners mostly used Shiner Price's boatyard at the Black Bridge. He worked out a way of getting the boats up the bank and back down again using two sets of sloping lines with a six-wheel bogie running on each. The bogies had uprights that were spring-loaded so they bent down as the bogies passed under the bottom of the boat and then came up again. At the top of the bank were two winches with wires running down to the bogies, and as the men started winding, the boat was caught by the uprights and pulled up the bank. There was another boatyard with a similar system of rails and winches just below Westgate Bridge, and boats were built there as well as being repaired.

Instead of paying a boatyard, it was possible for an owner to make use of a slipway on the Quay and do a simple repair himself. The main slipway opposite the bottom of Quay Street had a smooth ramp on either side with steps up the centre. Each ramp was wide enough for a longboat to fit on, but you needed a big tide to get her three parts of the way up or else there would be too much hanging over and she could break in half. You had to do the repair while the tide was down and get it all finished and tarred, and when it was tide time again, you pulled her back off the slip. She had to come off on that next tide, or if the tides were getting smaller, she might get stuck for a fortnight.

*As well as the privately owned longboats, there were a number of barges operating on the river that were owned by individuals or small firms.*

Jacob Rice and Son had their own barges that brought grain from Avonmouth to the mills at Gloucester and Tewkesbury, and some was trans-shipped into their own longboats at Gloucester for other mills in the Midlands. They operated as a small version of the Severn and Canal Carrying Company, but there wasn't any real competition between the two firms as each had their own regular customers. Jacob Rice and Son gave up their longboats in 1926, but they continued to carry wheat in their barges *Britannia, Harriet, Spry* and *Wasp* which had once been sailing vessels.

Other barges belonging to independent operators carried grain from Avonmouth to Healings Mill at Tewkesbury, and one or two went to Townshend's Mill at Worcester. Most were towed everywhere by tugs,

A privately owned trow and two Severn and Canal barges under tow on the Gloucester and Sharpness Canal

but some like *Monarch, J. & A.R.* and *Emily Priscilla* still used their sails in the estuary in the 1920s. Regular traders in the early 1930s included *Morland, Ripple* and *Volunteer* owned by Benjamin Perry and Sons of Bristol, *Flower of the Severn* and *Gertrude* owned by William Galbraith of Bristol, and *Sunbeam* and *Water Witch* owned by the Halling family of Tewkesbury. *Monarch* was owned by Healings of Tewkesbury and *Abmill* was owned by Townshends of Worcester. Other regulars were *Dora* owned by the Butt family of Saul, *Effort* owned by David Warren of Frampton on Severn and *Twee Gesusters* owned by William Phillips of Gloucester. However, many of these old wooden barges went out of service in the mid-1930s when Healings introduced their own steel vessels.

As well as the barges which mainly carried grain, G.T. Beard and Mousell Chadborn had a large number of lighters that normally carried timber between Sharpness and Gloucester but sometimes went on up to Worcester. Timber is a light cargo, so not only was the hull of the lighter filled, but the timber was stacked up solidly 8 or 10 feet above deck level. This meant that a man steering at the tiller on the after deck wouldn't have been able to see where he was going, and so a special platform was formed at the back end of the huge load using planks from the cargo. The helmsman stood on the platform so he could see over the top, and he had an extra long tiller reaching from the rudder head right up to the platform. Even so he only had a limited view, so there had to be a man on the forward end of the cargo giving him directions when it came to passing through bridges or entering locks. The lighters were towed up to the basin just above Diglis Locks, where some timber was put ashore at the timber yard there and some was transferred into longboats to go on up the Worcester and Birmingham Canal.

One further group of vessels carried crude tar from local gasworks for distillation at Butlers Tar Works at the Parting. The motor barge *Kathleen* did a regular trip from Stroud gasworks, and it was one of the last vessels to work up the Stroudwater Canal. The motor barge *Carbolate* went to Worcester, but it was too big to go up the canal, so it moored just upstream of the entrance lock. Then a horse-drawn boat collected the tar from the gasworks beside Lowesmore Pound and brought it down to the river where it was pumped into *Carbolate*.

# Severn and Canal Transformation

In the early 1920s, the Severn and Canal Carrying Company was struggling to remain in business, and new investment was desparately needed to meet the growing competition from both the railways and road transport. This chapter, based on documentary sources, describes how the company was rescued from the brink of collapse and given a new life.

Traffic through Gloucester had been dramatically reduced during the First World War, and many of the boatmen had gone off to join the services. Although trade improved again after the war, some of the men preferred higher paid jobs ashore, and it was difficult to replace them as few newcomers were able to take to the work they hadn't been brought up to do. Also the state of the inland canals had been allowed to deteriorate, and some stretches had become too shallow to take a fully laden boat. In 1919, the Severn and Canal Carrying Company carried 21,000 tons up the Worcester and Birmingham Canal and 18,000 tons up via Stourport. However, even with the help of continuing wartime government subsidies, the company was operating at a loss. With the prospect of government control ending in 1920, some of the smaller shareholders indicated that they wished to sell their shares.

Agreement was soon reached with customers to raise carrying charges, but a proposal to raise towing charges on the river by 100 per cent caused more difficulties. Although the tugs were operated by Severn and Canal, they were owned by the Sharpness New Docks and Gloucester and Birmingham Navigation Company which could veto any increase. The Dock Company directors were concerned that the higher charges would adversely affect other carriers and hence the trade of the port. Agreements dating back several years gave Severn and Canal very favourable terms for leasing the tugs and also covered reduced tolls on the canal, low rents for warehouses and a credit guarantee at the bank.

Some directors did not want to make any more concessions, but after considerable discussions and negotiations, the Dock Company eventually agreed to the 100 per cent increase in towing charges as from November 1920 in return for a higher rent for the tugs.

Shortly afterwards, the Severn Commission also increased its charges. This double blow was fiercely opposed by the other carriers, and it wasn't long before one of the principle lighter owners hired his own tug to take timber up to Worcester. This forced Severn and Canal to reduce the towing charge, and competition from the railways led to another reduction in 1922, so that the rate settled out at only 25 per cent above its former value. In the face of this competition, it was clear that Severn and Canal was not going to be profitable unless there were major changes in the methods of working, but the directors were not united in their ways of achieving this.

More than half of the ten thousand £1 shares of Severn and Canal were held by the Dock Company whose directors wanted to encourage the use of the Worcester and Birmingham Canal which they owned. Their influence was limited, however, because the Staffordshire and Worcestershire Canal Company held a £10,000 mortgage and their nominee, Alfred Butler, was acting as Managing Director. The Dock Company directors considered buying all of the shares, but they were advised that even their existing holding was beyond their authority, and so they tried to sell their shares to another carrying company. Although no agreement could be reached, George Cadbury heard about the difficulties and offered to take up some new shares. He wanted to promote canals and encourage waterways traffic to provide competition for the railways as this would help keep transport costs down.

Cadbury Brothers invested £6,000 in 1923 and £2,000 more in the following year, and George Cadbury and Alan Marsden became directors of Severn and Canal. Initially the new money was put towards paying off the Staffordshire and Worcestershire Canal Company mortgage, apparently in an attempt by the Dock Company to get rid of Alfred Butler. However, Cadbury wanted Butler to continue as a director and, at an extraordinary general meeting in 1925, the independent shareholders sided with Cadbury, and Butler was re-appointed. This paved the way for Cadbury to take over as Chairman of Severn and Canal and push through the great changes that were to transform the fortunes of the company. Cadbury's policy was to go for expansion by modernizing the fleet and the cargo handling facilities in order to attract new sources of traffic. More capital was raised by the issue of debentures to Cadbury

Steam tug *Victor* in Severn and Canal livery towing up river

Brothers and the Staffordshire and Worcestershire Canal Company, and the money was used to buy the river tugs *Active*, *Victor* and *Alert* from the Dock Company in 1926. Severn and Canal also took over responsibility for their own horse towing on the Worcester and Birmingham Canal, which had previously been provided by the Dock Company for a nominal charge.

The development of new ways of operating was temporarily disrupted by the General Strike of 1926, when all traffic came to a stop. After a week, an attempt was made to send the tug *Victor* to Tewkesbury with two barges carrying grain for Healings Mill. The pickets persuaded the usual crew that they would be acting against union orders and they refused to go. Later in the day, word spread that a volunteer crew had been recruited, and a crowd of about 300 strikers assembled by Gloucester Lock. As the boats came out into the river, the strikers tried to prevent the check ropes being secured, but there was a strong force of police on duty, and the attempt was unsuccessful. As the boats started up the river, the crowd followed along the Quay, and one man was seen to throw stones, one of which hit the tug's steering shelter. Despite being warned, he followed the boats for some way up the river and threw more stones. Eventually he was arrested, and when he appeared in court, he was sentenced to fourteen days hard labour. No more attempts were made to take barges up the river until the strike was settled, and then it was necessary to increase the charges for towing because of the increased cost of coal.

After the strike, more changes were made to attract new business. The new Company Secretary, Ernest Bayliss, moved the headquarters of the company from Gloucester to Bridge Street, Birmingham to be in closer touch with the customers, and Charles Hinman became Traffic Manager based at Bristol. Staff and overheads were reduced, and a new system of payment for boatmen was introduced in 1927. This had the effect of reducing the men's wages by 16 per cent, and it provoked two strikes lasting a total of six weeks before the national union leader, Ernest Bevin, was involved in negotiating a settlement.

Also in 1927, *Motor Boat No. 1* was bought from the Anderton Company at Stoke-on-Trent, presumably at the instigation of George Cadbury whose firm already had several motor boats carrying cargoes between Bournville and the outlying factories at Frampton and Knighton. At the Birmingham warehouse, electric hoists were installed to facilitate the quick handling of cargoes, and a new weighing machine was provided to deal with the local metal trade. Finally, to meet concern

Motor boat *No. 1* at Gas Street Basin in Birmingham

about the long-term viability of the Worcester and Birmingham Canal, George Cadbury arranged for a group of Birmingham and Bristol traders to guarantee making good any operating loss up to an agreed limit.

Unfortunately, all these measures were still not sufficient to make Severn and Canal profitable in the face of severe competition from the railways, who had in turn to counter the growing threat from road transport. Severn and Canal were forced to cut their rates, and in 1928 George Cadbury approached the Dock Company again asking for reductions in tolls of between 30 and 50 per cent. The Dock Company directors realized that they had to do something to help, but initially they would only consider a 20 per cent reduction. However, Severn and Canal threatened to cease operation, and as the Severn Commission was also losing money, there was a danger that the whole waterway route would collapse. In the end therefore, the Dock Company agreed to a 40 per cent reduction in tolls on all through traffic from Sharpness to Birmingham. Even this was not enough to make Severn and Canal profitable, but it provided a breathing space while other developments took effect.

*Motor Boat No. 1* was successful, and a second one was purchased from the Anderton Company in 1928. Also Cadbury's agreed to add their four motor boats to the Severn and Canal fleet, and these were given the numbers 3 to 6. At the same time, Cadbury's passed over all the traffic that they usually carried. This meant that Severn and Canal crews took more chocolate crumb from Frampton to Bournville, and they also worked between Knighton on the Shropshire Union Canal and Bournville for a few years until this traffic was sub-contracted to Fellows Morton and Clayton. Cadbury's boats had powerful Bolinder engines that were capable of towing a butty, but they could only carry around 20 tons. Later, therefore, the engines were transferred to converted horse boats that could carry 25 tons. Meanwhile two other horse boats were converted to become *Motor Boat No. 7* and *No. 8*. The stern of each boat was cut away at the company's boatyard at Stourport, and a new counter was built in its place. At the same time, the height of the cabin was raised to improve the accommodation for the crew.

Another development was the adoption of a more vigorous approach to publicity by means of leaflets detailing services, display stands at trade shows and putting the firm's name in large letters on the canvas cloths of the canal boats. The publicity emphasized the advantages of direct water transport from the Bristol Channel ports entirely under the company's control, with landing charges, cartage and other costs being saved by taking goods overside from steamers. Three motor vessels and seven barges operated in the estuary, three tugs provided a regular service on the river and seventy longboats carried the cargoes through to the Midlands. The publicity noted that the company had warehouses at Birmingham, Stourport, Worcester, Gloucester and Bristol where traders' consignments could be stored. From these, deliveries could be made in small lots to individual customers as required using the company's own lorries and horse-drawn carts. As well as the large consignments normally handled, the company ran a weekly service for smaller parcels each way between Bristol and Birmingham. Goods dispatched on a Thursday were guaranteed delivery to the customer by the following Monday.

A separate development that was to have a profound effect on waterways traffic was the erection of oil storage tanks at riverside sites. The Medway Oil and Storage Company established a depot at Stourport, and Shell Mex established one at Worcester. Soon these were being served by the dumb barges *Loyaltie, Sinceritie, Cleprod No. 1* and *No. 2*, and the larger *Shell Mex 7*. All these barges needed towing up and down the river by the Severn and Canal tugs, and this highlighted the condition of the old tug *Alert* which was only used when really

Tanker barge *Cleprod No. 1* and longboat in Diglis Lock

necessary. To replace *Alert*, therefore, it was decided to buy a motor tug from Watsons of Gainsborough. *Enterprise* was delivered in 1930, and as further growth in traffic was expected, *Progress* was built as a copy by Charles Hill and Sons at Bristol in 1931. Even so *Alert* was still kept busy for another year, and she only retired when *Trustie* was brought in by Medway Oil as the regular tug for the tanker barges *Loyaltie* and *Sinceritie*.

Continuing Cadbury's policy of modernizing the fleet, the Traffic Manager, Charles Hinman, specified an entirely new type of vessel that was capable of going to sea sufficiently far to serve the Bristol Channel ports and was also able to navigate up the Severn as far as Stourport. The first of this type, *Severn Trader*, was built by Charles Hill and Sons at Bristol in 1932 to the detailed designs of Alan Peck. Her length of 89 ft, beam of 19 ft 10 in and loaded draught of 7 ft were controlled by the dimensions of the Severn locks. She could carry around 160 tons of cargo, and the hold was made as large as possible to accommodate bulky goods. A three-cylinder 120 hp lamp-starting Kromhout engine gave her a speed of over 7 knots, and this was controlled from the wheelhouse so there was no need for a specialist engineer in the crew. A smaller diesel engine worked the anchor winch and the derrick used for cargo handling. Her funnel, mast and wheelhouse could fold down, and she had special ballasting arrangements to help her pass under the fixed bridges in all but the most exceptional flood conditions. Another vessel of the same type, *Severn Transport*, was built in 1933, and their ageing predecessors, *Osric*, *Serlo* and *Atalanta*, were sold.

The new Severn and Canal motor barges could not pass through the canal locks into the basins at Worcester or Stourport, and so new trans-shipment facilities were required. In 1934, therefore, Severn and Canal started developing a riverside site about 1 mile below Stourport which became known as Redstone Wharf. A simple wooden jetty was constructed, but there was no shedding and the wharf was mainly used for metals which could be stored in the open or for goods that were immediately distributed by road vehicles. Nearby Walsh Graham established a timber yard where they could receive large consignments delivered by lighter and then take small loads on by road to their saw mill at Wolverhampton as required.

The investment in new vessels was accompanied by changes in the types of cargoes carried. Considerable quantities of wheat had previously been taken to the mills in the Midlands, but many of these were closing down in the face of competition from mills at the ports, and the

*Severn Trader* approaching Gloucester on her maiden voyage 1932

carriage of wheat decreased. Severn and Canal therefore set out to get more higher value cargoes on which higher rates could be charged. Merchants and importers were approached with details of the costs of bringing goods via Avonmouth instead of London or Liverpool, and there was a very good response, particularly from the big food importers. If they had a consignment arriving on a ship, they could pass over the papers, and Severn and Canal would deal with the customs, carry the goods up to their warehouse in Birmingham and then distribute to the shops in the area as required. To promote this business, a new Commercial Manager, Jacobus Thoenes, was appointed. Also, as Cadbury's interest developed, more consignments of cocoa beans came via Avonmouth, and ships were chartered to bring sugar direct to Sharpness where it had to be unloaded quickly and taken to Frampton. With increasing quantities of chocolate crumb carried to Bournville, the total traffic for Cadbury's grew to around 50,000 tons per year. This increased traffic started to generate profits at last, and gradually the accumulated deficit was wiped out.

The company's success in attracting new sources of business prompted further investment in motor longboats. Using the experience gained with the earlier motors, Charles Hinman specified a design with several novel features, and eight new boats were built by Charles Hill and Sons at Bristol during 1934–5. Although the bottoms were formed of the usual elm planks, the sides were made of welded wrought iron plates, giving more cargo space than an all-wooden construction. As the previous policy of towing butties had not been very successful, each new boat was fitted with a smaller 9 hp Petter engine for single unit operation. Unusually, this was placed at the stern of the boat, behind the living accommodation, again saving space. As a result of these measures, the new boats were capable of carrying 30 tons, compared with the 25 tons of their predecessors.

Also in 1935, Severn and Canal decided to expand their involvement in the carrying of petroleum products. For several years, the river tugs had been towing dumb tanker barges up to Worcester and Stourport, but the Yorkshire firm of John Harker had captured much of the growth in traffic using motor barges which could also tow their own dumb barges. Severn and Canal had tried this form of transport using *Severn Carrier* and *Severn Carrier II*, built by Charles Hill and Sons in 1933, and they realized it was the best way to operate. They therefore ordered new motor tankers from Hills, took over the dumb tankers that were already in service and negotiated contracts directly with the Power and Cleveland petroleum companies for carrying to their depots at Stourport and Worcester. *Severn Traveller* and *Severn Tanker* were delivered in 1935, and *Severn Rover* and *Severn Voyager* came two years later. *Loyaltie* and *Sinceritie* were renamed *Severn Venturer* and *Severn Pioneer*, and *Cleprod No. 1* and *No. 2* became *Severn Conveyor* and *Severn Commerce*. Around the same time, Hills were building more dry cargo barges. The motor barge *Severn Industry* and the dumb barges *Severn Eagle, Severn Falcon* and *Severn Hawk* were delivered in 1935, and the motor barge *Severn Merchant* followed a year later. All these were largely financed by issuing £12,000 worth of new shares and £12,000 of debentures, which were quickly taken up.

The growing use of motor barges to tow dumb barges caused some concern to the Dock Company as it was affecting the use of their tugs on the canal and in the estuary. Partly in response to this, and also recognizing the improved financial position of Severn and Canal, the Dock Company decided to reduce the rebate on through traffic to

*Severn Rover* squeezing under Westgate Bridge with ice on the river

Birmingham from 40 per cent to 25 per cent. Severn and Canal accepted this but asked for a concession to be applied for traffic to Stourport as they thought a lot more business could be attracted in this way. After considerable discussion, the Dock Company agreed in 1937 to a flat rate per ton on all traffic to Stourport in return for assurances about continued use of the Worcester and Birmingham Canal and about restrictions on towing dumb barges. Furthermore it was agreed to hold more meetings between the two companies in future to improve cooperation.

Severn and Canal also had discussions with the Staffordshire and Worcestershire Canal Company about enlarging their barge locks at Stourport, but these did not lead to such a happy outcome. The idea was to allow the new motor barges to get into the basin at Stourport and make use of the warehouses there, but when the Canal Company heard that the intention was still to forward goods by road, they lost interest. In 1938, Severn and Canal announced that the accumulated deficit had been wiped out and that the ordinary shares were expected to become profit carrying. A remarkable transformation had been achieved, thanks to the drive of George Cadbury and the innovations that were made by his managers.

# CHAPTER 7

# *Motor Tugs on the River*

*An early move in George Cadbury's plan to revitalize the Severn and Canal Carrying Company was the purchase of two motor tugs,* Enterprise *and* Progress *(both given the prefix* Severn *by 1934). They were smaller and more manoeuvrable than the steam tugs, and they only needed a crew of two.*

When *Enterprise* came, she had no wheelhouse – the company said they hadn't enough money for that, and they just offered to find us a mackintosh! So we bent some pipes to form a frame which we covered with canvas until, after about three years, they did build a proper wheelhouse for us. There were over sixty longboats and about twenty barges using the river, and we towed almost everything then. Every morning, a tug left Gloucester bound for Worcester and another came the other way. Depending on the traffic, there might also be a second tug in each direction which usually left soon after the first. Your normal work was from Gloucester to Worcester in one day and back to Gloucester the next day. If there was a lot of traffic, they sometimes wanted you to bring your tug back on the first day, but you never knew whether you'd be called back until you got to Worcester. Quite often you had to take boats on to Stourport, and you still had to get back to Gloucester on the second day. We didn't like that much because you were pumping away at full speed with the engine throbbing in your ear all day and you didn't get much extra pay.

Normally the tugs worked in turn like the boats. In the early days, you did about two trips a week, mostly to Worcester, but in later years you could do three or more trips a week and mostly to Stourport. Any of the tugs could go to Stourport, but if it was a dry season, they had to send the motor tugs which only drew 3 ft 10 in of water. The steam tugs drew over 6 ft, and they could be hitting the bottom. You got your orders the afternoon before. With a motor tug, you could be given up to six longboats or two barges, but you often just had a barge and one or two longboats. The *Shell Mex 7* tanker needed her own tug as she was a big hefty barge and one of the worst we took up the river. There were also times when we went solo – even if there was nothing to take up, you still had to go if there were boats waiting for a tug at Worcester to bring them back next morning.

In the early 1930s, we left Gloucester at 8 o'clock in the morning. The old boatmen had been brought up in the days when the Gloucester tugs only went to Worcester, and they didn't want to change. But as the years went by, the starting time kept getting earlier until it was often about 6 o'clock. If you were going to Stourport, you wanted to make an early start, and you also liked to start early for Worcester in case you had to return the same day. The motor tugs moored overnight in the Old Arm. In the morning, you took the tug into the lock and up to six boats could fit in too. As you locked down, you gave each boat a tow rope, and when the gates opened, you took the boats in tow. You could take up to four longboats in single file, but with any more they had to go in two lines or else they'd be so strung out it would take them too long to

Motor tug *Enterprise* at Gloucester before a wheelhouse was fitted

get into the locks. If you had a barge, that went first on the tug, with the boats behind usually split into two lines.

To avoid jerking the ropes as you started off, you'd go up the stretch slowly until each rope came out of the water. It took quite a pull to start a loaded boat, and if you went forward too fast, you could break the rope. As soon as the last rope was set up, somebody gave you a whistle, and then you put on the power. Some of the barges would swim well, but others were as though they had an anchor behind them. One of the worst was *Emily Priscilla* for Tewkesbury. If you had four boats behind her as well, it was enough to turn you off your breakfast! The Dutch barge *Twee Gesusters* carried twice the cargo of *Emily Priscilla,* and if you had her solo, you had to get out of the way with the tug or she could run over the top of you. *Lufa* was another Dutch barge, and she was such a good swimmer that when you were in plenty of water, it was almost as though you were running solo.

Leaving Gloucester, we used the standard length of tow rope behind the tug to get the boats round the sharp turns on this stretch of river, but this meant they were close to the boil of the propeller, and all that pressure of water hitting against the first boat slowed it down. You had to accept this for the first few miles, but once you were above the Parting, the river was wider and there was no trouble getting round any more bends so you could have plenty of rope. To be ready for this, you had put the standard tow-rope on to the slip hook and had shackled on an extra half length of rope which went on the main hook. When the last boat was out of the Parting, all you had to do was to ease up and release the slip hook to let that extra rope draw out. This made it easier for the boats to keep to one side out of the wash of the tug's propeller, and you could gain half an hour on the trip.

There were several places up the river where fishermen put nets across to catch salmon, and you gave a blast on your hooter long before you got to these places to warn them you were coming. The first salmon draft was just above the Parting, and there were others at Ashleworth, Apperley, Lower Lode, Sandy Point and just below the weir at Worcester. There were also several shallow places that we called fords where you had to slow down and just niddle her over. The worst was at Wainlode Hill where the river was eroding a cliff, and a number of boats had been loaded with stones and sunk in a line to protect the base of the cliff. When the river was low, you could see the stones just above the water, and bathers used to swim out to them. Some of the stones had come out of the boats on to the river bed, and so you kept your tug well clear or else you could hit something hard. In spite of this protection, the river was very shallow, and you could have a devil of a job to get some of the large barges through this stretch.

*Monarch* was one of the most awkward things we took to Tewkesbury as she flopped down in the water like an old duck. She was a big sailing vessel with her mast lowered down to get under the bridges, and she was usually well loaded. We also had trouble with *Shell Mex 7*. So as you approached the ford with one of these barges, you slowed down and got her short up to the tug. If you kept going at speed, you had less water underneath the barge, and she'd be pushing silt up in front of her, making it more difficult to get over. So you went dead slow, and then if she started to ground, you'd go like the dickens, weaving this way and that. With the short rope, the propeller was close to her, and the backwater was so tremendous that it washed away all the silt and made a channel for her to come through. Once you were past the Red Lion pub, you let her go back on a long rope again, and off you'd go.

Carrying on up the river, you kept going at full speed most of the time, and the throttle wasn't usually pulled back until you got to the next lock. When the river level was low, all you had to do was to steer the tug up the middle, and the boats kept to one side out of your backwater. The current was only about 3 miles an hour, so you wouldn't try to cut the corners much as you'd risk running ashore or hitting a submerged tree. If there was some fresh in the river, you could cut the corners, and you kept the tug over to one side so the boats could go in the slack water close to the bank. All the heart of a river runs close to the outside of a bend and the slack water is on the inside, so you had to cross over from one side to the other to stay cheating the river. The tug had to keep out more than the boats because if her propeller hit an old tree or something, it could be damaged or lost. With four boats in a single line, they all went in close to the bank, and the churning water from the tug's propeller went past them. But with six boats in two lines, you had three in the slack water and three out in the current. They had to keep out to let that backwater drive down between the two lines. It would be a gruelling day for you, but you had to put up with it.

As skipper of the tug, you sat on your stool for one hour after another. Occasionally you looked behind to check the boats because many of the steerers just went where they liked. If they got into your backwater or ran off into the current, you might 'toot toot' and shout to bring them back into the slack water. If a boat wandered in towards the bank and she went underneath the withy trees and all the canvas was ripped, that

Motor tug *Enterprise* towing a *Cleprod* tanker barge and a longboat up the river

was up to them. It would make them take more notice next time. The tug could change speed or pull over a bit to help, but it was very seldom a thing like that happened.

Approaching Tewkesbury Lock, you'd blow one long blast on the hooter at Lower Lode so they knew to get the lock ready. You couldn't see the gates until you got right into the cutting, and so they had a signal that showed above the trees. If a black ball was hoisted, you knew the lock was against you and you waited. When the signal was pulled down, you went like the dickens into that lock until you were about a length from the top gates, and you knew just whereabouts you had to reverse to stop before you hit the gates. In this way, you could get the boats coming into the lock one after the other – no trouble. If any boat couldn't get into the lock, you tied the tug up to some pegs in the balks of the top gates, and then all the boats could pull on their ropes to get the last one in.

In the early 1930s, you usually had a barge that needed to be dropped off at Healings Mill on the Avon at Tewkesbury. While in Tewkesbury Lock, the first boat's rope was taken off the barge and put on the tug's towing hook, and a short rope from the barge was put on to the tug's slip hook. As you approached the Avon entrance, the skipper of the barge knew where to steer off to the side, and at just the right time, your mate snatched the hook. Away went the rope with the barge, she'd shoot on into the Avon and then she was bow-hauled from there to the mill. This practice declined in 1933 when Healings started operating their own motor barge *Deerhurst* towing the dumb barge *Apperley*. These were built at Bristol by Charles Hill and Sons, and the following year they were joined by the dumb barge *Bushley*.

After passing under the Mythe Bridge, you could fill up your water tank from the river because between the bridge and Sandy Point, there are seven springs running into the bed of the river day and night. You dipped in a bucket and filled up the tank, and you were all right then for about a week. The crew got their drinking water there too, and some of the longboat men filled their water cans there as well. When you met another tug coming down with a tow, you knew they'd be keeping to the middle of the river. If you wanted to pass on the left-hand side, you'd blow one blast for port, and if you were over the other side, you'd blow two blasts for starboard. You had right of way, but they wouldn't move over much – they liked to stay near the middle. You kept a special lookout approaching a ford, because the channel often wasn't wide enough for two tows to pass. They would be coming down twice as fast as you were going up, so you might have to give way. You just gave a blast or two as they came round the corner, and you stopped where you were just ticking over until they'd gone by.

At Upton upon Severn, the bridge was not very high and the left hand section could be swung off [i.e., open for boats] if necessary. But you had all the current coming down that side and you'd be crawling along there. So to save time when the river was low, you usually kept over to the other side as close to the bank as possible, and then you had a good run in slack water right up past Hanley Castle. The motor tugs usually had about 2 or 3 ft clearance under the bridge, but when it was half bank full, you had to lower the chimney and take the top of the wheelhouse off. The steam tugs had a very high funnel, and the crew always had to lower it down on to the engine casing, and then hoist it up as soon as they'd gone through. If there was some fresh in the river, they took the pin out of the funnel, put two ropes round it and rolled it off the casing down on to the deck. At Pixham near Kempsey, there was a chain ferry, and you always gave it a blast about a quarter of a mile before you got there. You had to give them plenty of warning because, once they were across, they had to let all their loose chain out so you could go over the top of it.

Motor tug *Enterprise* bringing a *Cleprod* barge into Diglis cutting

Approaching Diglis Locks at Worcester, you'd blow one long blast on the hooter to tell the lock-keeper you wanted the big lock. If you had so many boats that you wanted the two locks, you'd blow two blasts. As at Tewkesbury, you went into the lock as fast as you could to bring the boats in behind you. Leaving Diglis Locks, if you had a tanker barge or a timber lighter, you first took that into the basin just above the locks. A member of their crew went ashore at the lock, and as you approached the basin, he threw a line to the barge so they could get a check rope on to a post on the corner as it was such a sharp angle to get round. You took the tug steadily into the basin, keeping the barge moving in, and the check rope helped ease her round. You kept niddling her in and took her right alongside the quay wall. The Shell Mex berth was first on the right, and the second length up was for Cleveland. *Cleprod No. 1* and *No. 2* usually carried for Cleveland, but they also carried for Shell sometimes. The timber lighters went on the other side of the basin.

Sometimes you had the barge *Abmill* which was the only one we regularly took up for Townshend's Mill on the Worcester and Birmingham Canal. You took her up to Danny Watton's bottom lock at the entrance to the canal, let her drift up to you and got her alongside the quay wall just beyond the lock. Then you came alongside her and put a short rope off your hook on to her stern, and you both drifted back slowly with the current. When her bow passed the entrance to the lock, you got your tug moving ahead again, and she swung round into the lock quite easily. Once the barge was up in the basin, a line was run out, and she was winched up to Townshend's Mill. A small boat was kept for the purpose just above the locks. One of the crew rowed across the basin and put the rope round a post on the first corner, and they used the winch on the barge to heave her across. Then he ran the line up the tow-path to a post by the bridge, and they winched her right up underneath the elevator of the mill. While all this was going on, you went back and took the longboats for Birmingham up to Danny Watton's bottom lock so they too could work up into the canal basin.

If there were some boats for Stourport, you took them on as far as you could go while it was light. Otherwise you tied up underneath Danny Watton's wall and waited for a telephone message from the foreman at Gloucester. Sometimes you had to go back to Gloucester that afternoon, but usually you were told just to take empty boats down in the morning, and then you could tie up for the night. You could tie up alongside Danny Watton's wall, but often we went just upstream and ran the bow of the tug ashore on what we called the Gravel. This was a good place for catching eels using a long line with about ten hooks on. You baited all the hooks, chucked them over the side and tied the line to the chain of your steering gear. As soon as an eel took the bait, the chain rattled against the side of your bunk, and you went out and hauled him aboard. We had some beautiful eels there, often as big as your wrist. From there it was a mile to walk up into town, so sometimes we took the tug up a short distance above Worcester Bridge on the St John's side, and then it was only just over the bridge for us to go into the town. But when the river was high, it wasn't safe to be tied at the bridge because vandals could come and cut your ropes, and it would only be a matter of seconds before the tug would crash into the bridge. Then you either tied up by Danny Watton's wall or went down into the lock cutting.

A tug's normal work was to go from Gloucester to Worcester in one day and back to Gloucester the next day, but if you had any boats for Stourport, you took them on as far as you could before it got too dark. The old boatmen didn't like going far when it was dark, so you all agreed where you were going to stop, and it had to be near a pub. In the winter, you probably tied up in the cutting of one of the locks above Worcester. There you'd be safe even if the river rose or dropped. There was one pub near Camp [Bevere] Lock, and there were two at Holt Lock

Motor tug towing a lighter and four longboats up the river

– one on either side of the bridge. But there was no pub near Lincomb Lock unless you went right up to Stourport, and that's a long way to walk! If there was a lot of fresh in the river and you had a big tow, you might only get as far as Worcester on the first day. Then the next day, you went on to Stourport and back to Gloucester. In the summer, you generally reached Stourport on the first day, and you could often get back to Worcester by about 8 or 9 o'clock, when you'd tie up for the night.

The locks above Worcester are smaller than those below, and you could only fit in two longboats together with a tug. You had to get the two boats in first, and then the bow of your tug went up between their sterns. So you went into the cutting almost at full speed and then slowed the tug down to let the boats come up past you. As they went into the lock, you followed in behind. When the lock was filled and the gates opened, you could push the boats out steadily, and as soon as there was room for you to go past, you gave them your tow rope and away you went.

If you had three boats, you needed two lockings. You let the first two boats go in, and you waited below the bottom gates with the third boat. The first two boats had to shaft out of the lock or the lock-keepers might pull them out with a rope. To save time, you climbed the ladder on the outside of the bottom gates and opened the paddles to draw the lock off. We used to draw 3 or 4 ft of paddle up by the time the upper gates came to, and this caused them to close with a crash which the lock-keepers didn't like! Then we took the tug and the third boat through the lock, picked up the first two and carried on. If you had a barge, there wasn't room for the tug as well, and so you needed two lockings again. This time you took the tug through first and waited above the top gates. Then they ran a rope from the barge along the lock wall and in between the gates down to the tug. When the bottom gates opened, you moved the tug forward to pull the barge into the lock, and the rope remained on the tug so that when the top gates opened, away you could go.

In the early thirties, the tugs went right up to Stourport and tied up in the river outside the public house called the Tontine Hotel. But this took up so much time that Severn and Canal based a small motor tug called *Margo Newman* at Stourport, and then the Gloucester tug didn't usually go through Lincomb Lock. The lock-keeper at Holt rang through and told them when to expect us at Lincomb, and the *Margo Newman* was always there ready. She took on the barges and boats we had brought up, and we picked up anything that had to go back to Gloucester.

One time, we did have to go through Lincomb Lock to help recover two longboats carrying steel pipes and girders that were stuck on Lincomb Weir. They had been moored abreast at Redstone Wharf, and some kids must have chucked off the ropes during the night. When the boats hit the weir, the pressure of the water built up along the side of one boat, and it ran over the top because it had no side cloths on. As one boat filled up, it took the other down as well, although there wasn't enough depth for the boats to go right under. To get them up, we brought a barge alongside and fitted a big balk across from the barge to a strong trestle over the weir. We got a wire underneath one boat and we used a winch to lift it up until we could get in wearing waist boots. We got on top of the steel and started lifting it out into the barge. The steel was very heavy, and it wanted three or four of you on each length. When we'd picked up so much, they moved the wire back further until it got to the middle of the boat, and the more we got out the higher the boat was lifted. At the same time, we had a pump working like the dickens to pump out the water, and after a few hours we got both boats up.

Going down the river, the boats were usually empty so there was no need for the big ropes, used when loaded boats were going uphill. Instead they used their own ropes that were specially supplied for towing on the river. You always made sure they had good ropes because you knew the difficulty you'd be in if one broke. If you had a barge, that came immediately behind the tug, and the boats followed in pairs on short cross ropes so they'd just miss the barge's rudder. If you had a loaded boat, that came last on a long rope, and it helped to hold the other boats straight.

Motor tug *Progress* towing *Nelson* and other barges

Coming through Worcester, you had to get your orders from Danny Watton, the lock-keeper at the entrance to the Worcester and Birmingham Canal. When you were early enough to keep on going to Gloucester, you just gave a couple of long blasts on the hooter as you passed the cathedral, and Danny Watton came out of his office and signalled to you. If it was all right for you to carry on, he'd wave towards Gloucester, you'd 'Toot Toot' and off you'd go. But if there were some boats in the basin and he wanted you to stop, he'd put his two hands up. Then you took your tow down into the cutting, turned the tug around and brought her up alongside Danny Watton's wall. Once the boats had locked down, you took them to join the others in the cutting.

When you were going to stay overnight at Worcester, you got your boats tied up alongside Danny Watton's wall, and then you put the tug on the Gravel or took it up above the bridge for the night. In the morning, we liked to make an early start, and if there were some boats to collect from the basin, you might have to pop up and kick the side of the cabins to wake them up. Then you worked the boats down through the locks while the crews were getting dressed. You knew the lock-keepers at Diglis were on at 6 o'clock, so you wanted to give them a blow at a quarter past and then you were home for dinner.

As you came under the Mythe Bridge, you might see by the bank ahead of you a barge that needed picking up and taking to Gloucester. When a barge was discharged at Healings Mill, they bow-hauled her out on to the main river and held her there with a rope round a post and back to the barge so they could release it easily. You took the tug past the entrance to the Avon very slowly, and when you were nearly alongside the barge, you reversed the engine so the boats behind on short ropes came up on either side of the stern of the tug and stopped. You wanted that barge close up behind the tug, so the boat crews chucked their ropes aboard the stern of the barge, and you went forward to catch a rope off the bow of the barge. By the time you'd got that rope on your hook, the boatmen whistled to say their ropes were all right, and away you went into Tewkesbury Lock.

At the Parting, you had to turn off the main channel into the Gloucester water, and when there was some fresh in the river, you relied on all your experience to know just what your tug had to do to bring the boats in safely. If the boats were allowed to snake about, they could break a rope and go off down towards Maisemore Weir. So approaching the Parting, you went into the slack water on the Sandhurst side and you slowed down as much as possible without letting the ropes go slack. Just before the Parting, you brought your tug out to

Motor tug *Progress* and tanker barge *Severn Traveller* by Gloucester Quay with the river in flood

avoid the dead water on the point, and as you were brushing the main current, you turned into the Gloucester water and wound your tug up to full speed. The slower you were going before the turn, the better it was for bringing all the boats round with you and avoiding any slack ropes.

At Gloucester, a motor tug could take a few boats straight into the lock if it was ready. You slowed the tug down to keep in very close to the Quay wall, heading for the left side of the lock, and just before you got to the gates, you felt the tug starting to heave off due to the current going down to the weir. If you judged it right, this would leave the tug heading straight for the lock, and as her bow entered, you wound her up and brought in the boats behind you. You could only bring in four boats like this – with any more, the last ones would have been left outside and carried round the corner by the current. If you had six boats in the tow, the last two had to cast off and get a line ashore. So as you came by the Quay, you put your tug in reverse and held the boats back until somebody jumped up on to the wall. He took a line off the last two boats and held them back while you took the first four into the lock. Then the other two were bow-hauled down to fit in beside them. This wasn't difficult with empty boats.

# CHAPTER 8

# *Bores and Freshes*

*There can be very large tides in the Severn Estuary and anything over 23 ft at Sharpness is enough to come over the weir at Llanthony, just below Gloucester. A big tide will run all the way up to Haw Bridge; the reduction in downward flow beyond there being enough to raise the water 2 to 3 ft up the weir at Tewkesbury. The river level can also change rapidly after heavy rain, and a tug skipper had to know how to cope with whatever conditions he found.*

As a big tide funnels up the estuary it forms a wave known as the bore, and this could push your tow boats all over the place. The main tide rushes up the Maisemore channel [to the west of Alney Island], and as it sweeps past the Upper Parting some of the water turns back towards Gloucester. A few minutes later, the tide also comes up the Gloucester channel [to the east of Alney Island], and the two meet just above the Black Bridge. As skipper of the tug, you had to know if a big bore was due or else you could risk a rope breaking or a boat being damaged. If a big tide was due soon after you were leaving Gloucester Lock, you got all the boats moored along the Quay and waited for the Gloucester water to go by. You strung them out along the wall with their towing ropes slack and each with a stern rope out. Once the tide had gone past, you took your tug up to the stretch with all the ropes tight, and when they let go the stern ropes, away you went like the clappers!

If the tide was later, you tried to arrange to be approaching the Parting as the bore came up the Maisemore channel. When the water turned down the Gloucester channel, it almost stopped you dead, and you had to be ready with the controls so that you could ease up as the ropes went slack and then go full throttle when the ropes came taut again. You wanted to meet the bore within a few hundred yards of the Parting because, with three or four boats on, you couldn't make much headway and you had to keep banging away to get out into the main channel.

Then you probably got that tide helping you all the way to the Haw Bridge. You never went out of the Parting just before the main bore because it would wash you all over the place. If you thought you were well enough ahead to risk it, you were on tenderhooks hoping it wouldn't be early. For a big tide, you always allowed an hour from the time of high water at Sharpness until it reached the Parting, but if there was a strong wind blowing with it, the bore could be a quarter of an hour earlier. So you got a tired neck looking behind to see whether it was coming and you needed to slow down. When the wave did come, each boat was pushed forward like a surf rider nearly up to the boat in front, and then it settled back. You saw each boat rise up and you knew when it was your turn. Once the wave had gone past the tug, you wound her up steadily until you could see each rope come up out of the water and you all got straightened out. When all the ropes were taut, you could go full speed again.

Similarly, when coming downstream and a bore was due, you kept a look out for it once you were below Ashleworth. When you saw it coming, you slowed down so there wouldn't be too much jerk on the ropes. Slowing down was especially important if you had a loaded boat in the tow because if you were moving fast and it got caught under the bore, it would dive and it might not come up. After the bore had gone past the stern of the first longboat, then you could start pulling again. You always made sure you were not at the Parting when the bore got there or else it could knock you for six!

Working on the river could also be a bit tricky after heavy rain, particularly when coming downstream, but you kept out of trouble by doing what you'd learned from the old tug skippers and from your own experience. Coming down the river when it was half bank full, you had to be careful taking the longboats into the still water in the cuttings. Well before a lock, you put your tug dead slow – you were still going down the river at a good speed, but the ropes were hanging in the water and you were only just giving the boats steerage way. Just as the tug was going to hit the still water in the cutting, you wound her up to full speed ahead and pulled the boats in too. Otherwise, the tug would almost have stopped in the dead water while the river carried the boats straight into the island or round and over the weir. When there was 6 ft of fresh in the river, you didn't have to worry about the cuttings as you could go over the weirs and you could get home very quickly. You knew when you could go over the weirs because you had certain marks you had learned from the older skippers. You could also go upstream over the weirs when you only had one barge in tow. This saved going through the lock, but I don't know whether we gained any time because it was very very slow going upstream. While you were going past the lock, you could fry a piece of bacon, eat it and wash up – it was murder.

Going up and down the river nearly all your life, you got to know almost every tree. You could look at a tree that was once a thin withy and think 'I remember you when you were only a stick.' Even if there was a flood all over the land from Stourport to Gloucester, you knew where the river was by keeping an eye on the trees. We never stopped for darkness or floods – we always got where we wanted to be, and I never knew a tug get lost and run into a meadow. One time when the river was bank full, we had to come down at night so we could tow something out the next morning. We were gassing down at 10 or 12 miles an hour, and it was black as a bag. I could just about recognize the trees, and I had to use all my instincts to know where the river was. We never went through a lock, but we gave the lock-keepers a 'Beep Beep' as we went over the weirs – just to let them know we'd gone by!

You were always learning on the River Severn, and you had to be prepared for anything. One day *Enterprise* was towing three boats upstream and they were keeping well into the side as there was a certain amount of fresh water in the river. Suddenly, as we were approaching Ashleworth, the first boatman shouted that he was sinking. The boat had hit a concrete outlet to a drain that was 3 ft under water, and he was taking in water fast. I knew the only thing to do was to get him on the shelving bank right opposite the pub at Ashleworth, so we gave him a good start and he ran up on to that. The other two boats also went into the bank and tied up to trees as best they could.

I took the boatman's wife and two kids off and raced the tug back to Gloucester with them to report what had happened. The foreman got a spare tug and took an empty barge up to Ashleworth. He moored the barge alongside the damaged boat and put two balks of timber over the boat from the high side of the barge on to the bank. He sank a wire down underneath the bow and up to a winch, and they started heaving up and heaving up until we could get a tarpaulin over the hole to stop any more water entering. Then the pumps on the tug and on the barge were used to pump the water out. The boat had a load of lead on for Birmingham, and now it had to be unloaded. Luckily we had one boat in the tow which was only half full, and so we all started chucking the lead on to this other boat, and the rest went on to the deck of the barge. Then we took the damaged boat back to Gloucester alongside the barge, and they put her in the small dry dock for repair. The other boats stayed where they were overnight, and crews used the salmon fishermen's boat to get across to the pub for a drink, so they were quite happy!

A more serious accident occured because of the difficulty of getting through Worcester Bridge when the river level was high due to the arches of the bridge holding the water back and causing strong eddies. *Active* was coming down with a loaded coal boat on a long rope, and the boat was carried through a different arch to that used by the tug. The tug's crew couldn't release the towing line as they were all forward waiting for the crouch as they squeezed under the bridge and, as the rope set up, it pulled the boat sideways and ripped half of her deck off. The crew were thrown overboard, and although the woman and little boy were saved, the skipper was drowned. His body was carried well downstream, and it was only recovered eighteen months later when the dredger was digging for sand opposite Worcester Cathedral.

*Active* was involved in another incident at Worcester when the river level rose four feet in one night. *Enterprise* was tied up alongside the top end of the wall below Danny Watton's lock, and *Active* came up after us and tied on to a post upstream with her stern overlapping our bow and

Steam tug *Active* at the second lock on the Worcester and Birmingham Canal, the entrance lock in the background being under water

protruding out into the stream. As the river rose during the night, we heard a crunching noise going on as the current was rocking the steam tug against our bow, and it was putting a great strain on the mooring post. Eventually the post pulled out of the ground just as me and my mate were getting up the next morning. *Active* could have drifted over the weir, but as it went by, I ran out of the cabin and grabbed the rope that was dangling down with the post still in it. I kicked the post clear and put the eye of the rope on to our bollard. As the rope set up, it broke, but it checked the drifting tug into the slack water just below the lock entrance. By this time the crew had woken up, and they threw me another rope which I put on to our post. Then I went back to finish dressing as I hadn't any trousers on!

When there was a lot of fresh in the river, it made towing upstream much more difficult – particularly turning into the main river at the Parting. The worst thing we took up was the tanker barge *Shell Mex 7*, which was a big hefty thing and always had her own tug. The usual skipper insisted on using a short rope so the tug would help him round the bends, but if that big craft made a run, she took a small motor tug like *Enterprise* where she wanted to go. You could turn your wheel, but because the tow rope was so short, the tug didn't answer, and the further you went the more you tilted over. One day there was a lot of fresh in the river, which had raised the level 6 ft at Worcester, and we had trouble going round the turn at Enstones [the Globe public house]. The skipper wouldn't pull the wheel over hard enough to help get her round, and so she went straight into the bank. That brought the tug up with such a jolt that the cooking range shifted right across the cabin floor and the pots and pans fell with a crash! We couldn't pull her away forward, so we had to reverse with the ropes, pull her back out of the bank and have a new start.

After that, I was worried what might happen turning into the main river, so I told my mate to sharpen the axe and stand by the hook. At the Parting, it was like a big whirlpool going round, and the fresh water coming down was creating a boil. It was dangerous to have two longboats on there, let alone this big thing with over 300 tons in, and short up to the tug at that. As we started turning, the tanker skipper expected the tug to pull him round, and we tilted so badly that water started coming in through a porthole – all over our beds and all over the floor. So I told my mate to cut the rope, and as the tug suddenly came upright, the catch came off the cupboard door and cups, saucers, tea, sugar and condensed milk were flying all over the place – it was a proper mess! The tanker ran straight up the bank on the other side, and the crew gave me all the foulest language you ever heard – it's a wonder the heavens didn't send for me. While they were giving me all this fire, I just let the tug drift back and told them to give me another rope. The next day, I had to go and see my boss and one of the Shell Mex people. I explained what had happened, and it got settled all right without us having to pay for a rope or anything. They told the tanker skipper to use a longer rope in future, and then there was no more trouble.

Normally you could get to Stourport in one long day, but if there was a lot of fresh in the river, it could take much longer. Once *Enterprise* had to take two barges loaded with copper and aluminium which was wanted urgently at Stourport. The river wasn't quite half bank full when we started at about 10 o'clock at night, but there had been a lot of rain, and they reckoned it rose 9 ft in the next few hours. We kept pumping away all night, taking it in turns to get a bit of sleep, but the current was so strong that by 6 o'clock next morning, we had only just got into Tewkesbury cutting. We eventually reached Diglis Lock late that evening, and I told one of the skippers to tie up above the lock while I took the other barge on to Camp Lock. We could just get under Worcester Bridge, and by keeping in the slack water as much as possible, we got to Camp in reasonable time. As soon as we'd started the barge into the cutting, we whipped round and came back to Worcester in no time to pick up the second barge. The water was still rising, and I wondered if we would get under Worcester Bridge this time. I had my mark at the Race Course, and I could see it would be touch and go. As we went for the bridge, the action of the propeller drew the water away, and we dropped down and just got under. We picked up the second barge and then had to come back through the bridge again. The worry this time was whether they would keep the barge true into the bridge hole or whether they would scrape the side and pull us back, but they were very good and we got through.

When we reached Camp, the first barge had been locked up, and they locked us up with the other one. Again we took one barge on to Holt and came back for the second, and then we did the same between Holt and Lincomb. This meant another night with only a couple of hours sleep each, and we got the second barge to Lincomb just after dinner on the third day. The *Margo Newman* took the barges on from there and we breathed a sigh of relief. We chased back, coming over all the weirs and just scraped through Worcester Bridge all right. We tied up alongside Danny Watton's wall, looking forward to a good night's sleep, when the message came for us to go back to Gloucester. I felt like telling the foreman to come and fetch the tug himself, but we had to put up with it! We got back to Gloucester about 10 o'clock that night, and we had another tow at 6 o'clock the next morning.

On one trip back from Stourport, the river was so high that *Enterprise* couldn't get through Worcester Bridge and we were trapped there for about four days. Coming down the flooded river, I had noticed a place where there were many rabbits in the hedgerows because everywhere else was under water. We had bags of time to waste, so without telling anybody, we took the tug back up over Camp Weir and on to where I had seen the rabbits. We went ashore with a Cadbury's crumb sack, and within an hour we had collected about sixty rabbits making the sack so full we had a job to get it on board again. Back at Worcester, there were six longboats in Diglis Basin, and we gave them enough rabbits for their meals. The next day the river had gone down a bit, and so I filled our tanks up with water and dropped her down through the bridge stern first. We only just got through, and some of the paint was scraped off the top of the engine casing. The boats in our tow had to stay above the bridge because their cabins wouldn't go underneath. When we got back to Gloucester, we still had plenty of rabbits, and we gave most of them to our friends and neighbours.

If the river was high, you needed the bridge at Upton upon Severn swung off, and it was quite tricky getting through the narrow opening. As soon as you could see the bridge, you sounded your hooter, and there was always somebody there to get it ready for you. The opening section was on the Upton side where all the current was. Going upstream you started by keeping the tug in the middle of the river, and then you moved her across gently to get in line with the swing section, so the boats went through the bridge like a snake. You had to keep going full speed all the time to keep the ropes taut and help the boats get through the narrow opening, but you were only going at crawling speed, and it seemed you were in that bridge for ages.

When going downstream, you had to be very careful, and you gave some blasts on the hooter about half a mile before the bridge so they started to get it off. You kept in the slack water close to the Upton side, going very slowly so the ropes were only just pulling, and as you got to the bridge, you gave full throttle to bring every rope up tight. Then you heaved off to dive through the centre of the opening, and each of the following boats put their tiller hard over to bring their stern round to help the next one through. It all happened very quickly, and you had to make sure you got it right because a big barge could have damaged the bridge.

In 1939, the old bridge was replaced by a new higher level bridge, and Severn and Canal helped transport some of the girders. The two girders intended to form the central span were loaded on to *Encore*, a long flat-topped barge normally used for salvage work at Sharpness, and they were towed up river by *Severn Victor*. The two side spans of the bridge were already in place, and the barge was brought up through the opening, swung round and allowed to drift back so she could anchor in the middle. Two steam hoists lifted each girder up, but as they were lowering the second one into place, the wire on the Upton side started to break, and as each strand failed it was like a cannon firing. It only had a little way to be lowered and everybody was on tiptoe. We were sweating and we were doing nothing – just standing by. The old foreman was trembling as he shouted out the orders to keep lowering. If they had stopped, it would have given that extra jerk and the girder would have gone to the bottom of the river. It was nearly in place, when suddenly the last strand went bang, and the marvellous thing was it dropped straight in to a proper fit. We thought that something might have happened to the part of the bridge that was already there, but fortunately all was well.

*Severn Victor* bringing the girders for Upton Bridge

The main obstacles to traffic when the river level was high were the two bridges at Gloucester – the Black Bridge and Westgate Bridge. If it was too risky for empty boats to make a run for it, they turned round where there was an inlet in the bank we called the swinging hole, and they dropped through the bridges stern first. The steam tugs left the boats to manage this on their own, but a motor tug was sufficiently manoeuvreable for you to be able to help them.

If there were any loaded boats in the tow that could get under the bridges easily, you ran straight through with them first. Passing the Jolly Waterman, you let go the ropes of the empty ones, picked up the loaded ones and took them down to Gloucester. They dropped alongside the Quay and were bow-hauled into the lock. Meanwhile you swung the tug into the bank and went back up to help the empty boats which had turned round on their own and were drifting down on the pig. If you only had empty boats in the tow, you could all turn round together. You went into the bank and let the current swing the tug round. The first two boats slackened their ropes so they drifted past the tug, and then the ropes were checked to pull their bows round. As they turned into the bank, the boats behind slackened their ropes and turned in too. Then you pointed the tug upstream, and as all the boats lined up behind, you just kept niddling to steady them as they drifted backwards down through the bridges.

You could easily move them to one side or the other because a kick on your propeller made the water go past them faster, and so their rudders had more effect. To give them even more control, they also threw a line ashore to one of the crew who had jumped off at the swinging hole. He normally just held the line in check, but if the swirl of the water coming down towards the bridge was heaving the boats over the other side, he could pull them back. At Westgate Bridge, you could hold them against the stream, and the men could push with their hands to get the boats lined up right to go under the middle of the arch. Then you eased the tug down and gradually drifted back until you all passed through the bridge, and you went on dropping backwards down to the Quay. Beyond the end of the Quay wall was a sloping earth bank, and it was wide enough there for each boat to swing round on a rope. Then when the lock was ready, you caught hold of the boats and towed them into the lock in the usual way.

The steam tugs couldn't do all this as they were more awkward, and they used to leave the boats and go through the bridges on their own. They took the funnel down and rolled it off the casing, and the engineer

*Progress* and *Enterprise* outside Gloucester Lock with the river level high and the floodgates closed to protect the water level in the dock

pumped some water into the bilges. Then the wheel was the highest point, and when I was on *Victor*, I saw what old Chick Thomas used to do about this. Coming down towards Westgate Bridge, he said to the engineer down the speaking tube 'Give her all you've got!' and he loosened the nut holding the wheel. We were going a tremendous speed, and as the bow of the tug was entering the bridge, he whipped the wheel off and ducked down. He held the wheel in his hand until the tug had skimmed through the bridge, and then he put it back on ready for the sharp turn that followed. It was a smart job and a thrill to watch!

To help barges get under the bridges, their wheelhouses were designed to be stripped down, but if the water was more than about 16 ft above the sill of Gloucester Lock, it was too risky to take empty barges through Westgate Bridge, so they had to tie up. Just above the Black Bridge was a bend where the bank was cut away – as kids we used to go swimming there and dive off that bank. The barges could moor there without coming to any harm if the water went up or down, and there were special posts for them to tie to. Meanwhile you carried on with any longboats, and you dropped them through the bridges stern first.

We never had to leave any longboats above the bridges, because if it was that bad they didn't come. You telephoned down from Worcester to ask what the water level was at Gloucester Lock, and you looked at your tide book to see if the tide would be pushing it up further. If the water was going to be more than 22 ft above the sill of the lock, you all stayed at Worcester, or if you wanted a change, you came down to Tewkesbury and tied up by Healings Mill. But as *Enterprise* wasn't as high as a longboat, there were times when you left the boats at Worcester and brought the tug down on its own, so at least you could sleep at home that night. Knowing that you barely had room to get under Westgate Bridge, you stripped the funnel and everything down as low as you could, and you had the throttle wide open. As the tug went into the bridge hole, the action of the propeller drew the water away from the sides of the bridge so you sunk down and got an extra few inches of clearance. By the time you came back up again, you'd gone through the bridge. It was a thrilling job as you had to be coming at such a speed that the tug's name was only just showing above the water, and you had to go under the middle of the arch where there was most headroom.

Another natural difficulty affecting traffic on the river was ice, although it never stopped the boats in my time. One year when the water was really low and there was hardly any stream, it started to freeze at Llanthony weir and it slowly spread all the way up to Wainlode Pool above Ashleworth. You only had to drop a rope in the water, and as you lifted it out it had icicles on it. A tug going up the river broke a channel through the ice, and within twenty minutes, a thin sliver of ice formed on it again. As all the vessels passed up the same channel, they pushed the ice to the side, and it got thicker there until it was 9 or 10 in thick, but the boats could still get through. One bit that did freeze solid was the entrance to the Avon leading up to Healings mill at Tewkesbury. Their motor barge *Deerhurst* only went up occasionally, and from the mill to the Severn it was 6 in thick. We had to take *Progress* up there and break it up for them. We went into the ice until it stopped us, and we came back and made another charge. Each time we only went forward a few yards, and then we had to reverse and have another go. We kept doing this for hours, and we had no paint on the bow afterwards – just shiny plates.

# CHAPTER 9

# *Motor Boats to Birmingham*

*Very soon after George Cadbury took control of the Severn and Canal Carrying Company, he arranged for the introduction of motor boats to replace some of the traditional horse-drawn longboats.*

Severn and Canal bought their first motor boat in 1927, and over the next two years they had seven more. *No. 1* and *No. 2* were known as Knobsticks as they were built by the Anderton Company of Stoke-on-Trent, and they had 15 hp Bolinder engines. *No. 1* was a very fast boat but would only carry 21 tons which wasn't big enough for Severn and Canal, so the design was altered for *No. 2* to make it carry 25 tons. *Nos. 3, 4, 5* and *6* were ex-Cadbury boats with the older water drip Bolinder engines. *No. 7* and *No. 8* were ex-Severn and Canal horse boats converted at the company's yard at Stourport. All five planks at the stern were taken out and new ones steamed in at different positions. The lower planks were drawn in to make the swim for the propeller, and the top two planks were extended out and round to make the counter. The older boatmen who had been with the company for many years were given the first choice of new boats, and they all went for the motor boats if they could get them. One drawback was that the counter cupboard had a tendency to get damp because of the water boiling up from the propeller. So we had to put our food in the cupboard over the side bed, and to keep butter and bacon cool, we had them outside wrapped in a fabric thing that we kept wet.

The ex-Cadbury boats were too small for Severn and Canal as they only carried 20 tons, so one at a time the engines were put into converted horse boats which were given the same numbers. At the same

131

The Bolinder engine in motor boat *No. 3*

time, the engines were converted to the new design to remove the water drip. The original Bolinder engines had fuel injection from the side, and when they were warm, you could put a spot of water in with each injection of fuel. The water and oil exploding together made you bolt ahead, but they found that the water was causing big scores in the cylinders so they had to stop it. Bolinders provided a conversion kit which included a domed piston and a new head that fitted round it having a hot bulb with injection from the top.

To start a Bolinder, you put your foot on a pin protruding from the fly-wheel and gave it a kick, but if you didn't get it right, it sometimes kicked back. They were all naughty at times, but *No. 6* was a terror as it was always kicking back. The skipper was only a little fellow, and one time it threw him straight out through the doors and into the canal! After that, he used to shut the doors. Then if he was thrown back, he'd knock the doors open and that would stop him being thrown out. To come astern, you had to change the whole engine into reverse. You pulled the reverse lever to cut the main fuel pump out, and just as the engine was on its last turn, the reverse pump hit once and the explosion drove the piston back the other way. As soon as you heard it change, you pushed the lever back to the neutral position. With some engines this change-over was unreliable, and it could just stop. If this happened as you were going into a lock at about 4 miles per hour, you had to be quick getting into the engine room and giving it a kick to get it going again, as you only had a few seconds to do it!

In the mid-1930s, Severn and Canal had eight welded iron longboats built by Charles Hill at Bristol, and they were all named after trees: *Oak, Ash, Elm, Fir, Pine, Willow, Beech* and *Alder*. Each had a 9 hp Petter engine with a gearbox that gave forward and reverse, and there was a brake band clutching system to help you come into mesh automatically. A feature unique to these boats was that the engine was astern of the cabin. This gave more headroom in the cabin compared with when the engine was in front and the floor had to be raised over the propeller shaft. But a disadvantage was that it made the cabin hotter because there was less fresh air. You only had a little slide in the top of the cabin and two port holes, and you never got enough fresh air unless there was a good breeze. During the same period, Severn and Canal converted two more horse boats, *Swan* and *Cork*, bringing the total number of motor boats to eighteen.

Going up to Birmingham with *No. 2* single, we took about 6 to 6½ hr to get to Worcester, and this applied almost whatever the condition of the river. When the river was in flood, we travelled slower but we saved time by going straight up over the weirs. You had to learn the way of doing this, because although the water looked level, it was going much faster over the top of the weir. If you charged up there with a loaded boat at full speed, at the top of the weir you'd go right under because you'd be hitting the full force of the water. So you went up steady until you reached the fast water, and then you turned the engine up full to go over the weir. Also we saved time by going straight into Danny Watton's top lock at Worcester – when his bottom lock was under water, he chained the gates back to keep them open.

One time in a high flood, I was up by the Rhydd above Upton when the motor tanker *Darleydale* came by and offered me a tow. I surprised the captain by saying 'Yes', and I threw him a rope. He couldn't half go, and he pulled my deck straight under water, pushing the bow wave well up the cratch. I knew this wouldn't sink her though, as when it was a flood, I always lashed a piece of canvas over my deck hatch to stop any water getting in. So he pulled me up to Worcester like that!

If there was a horse boat going to the same destination, the 15 hp Bolinders were supposed to provide a tow. If a horse boat went up with

Motor and butty at Worcester

the tug, Worcester was his first day, Tardebigge his second and it was 3 o'clock on the third day before he got to Birmingham. If he came up behind a Bolinder leaving Gloucester Lock at 6 o'clock in the morning, he could be near Stoke Prior that night and into Birmingham the next day. He was a day ahead, and he could save another day coming home. Going up on the tug, a horse boat took seven or eight days to do the round trip to Birmingham, but a Bolinder could have him home again in five days. The standard payment to Birmingham was 2s 3d per ton. A horse boat might have 33 tons in, but a motor boat could only take 25 tons. If you pulled him up the river and all the way to Birmingham, you had to wait and do everything for him, so in return they split the total payment between the two skippers.

When towing a butty, the more fresh water in the river, the longer it used to take going upstream, and I've been as many as 17 hr trying to get to Worcester. Then I roamed the river to keep in the slack water as much as possible – that's the art of going up the river. Because the current goes round the outside of a bend, you had to come up the slack water on the inside. There was never a rule to keep to one side in our day, and so you used the river as you needed. The down traffic gave way to the up, and you blew for whichever side you were going – one toot on your horn for port or two for starboard. When crossing the current, the motor was slowed down and the butty caught up in the slack water. You used 40 fathom of rope to let you get across into the slack water on the other side, and then the motor was pulling like hell as the butty swung across in the current behind you. Sometimes you were standing still until you got that butty across, and then you started to make way gradually ahead. In fact I've gone backwards crossing the river! You had to watch it if the rope went slack, but being 40 fathoms, it had a good spring in it when it came up taut again. The long rope also helped the butty keep out of the motor's water which made a big difference to the pulling.

The Bolinders were made for pulling a butty up the river, but we preferred to go on our own if we could. Even if there were horse boats waiting at Gloucester Lock, we often went on our own. It was the first boat on turn that was supposed to come with us, but if there was a drop of fresh water in the river, he thought he'd be quicker on the tug and he didn't want to loose his turn. The Petters could go up the river on their own, but they wouldn't take them up if the water level was more than 14 or 15 ft above the sill of Gloucester Lock. Then the tug pulled them or one of the Bolinders. If I was going up the river with my Bolinder and a friend of mine was coming out with a Petter, I'd put a rope on him and pull him to Worcester. It would make him an hour and a half quicker and slow me down an hour and a half. But if he wasn't a friend, I'd just leave him!

Once on the Worcester and Birmingham Canal, you could only go as fast as the depth of water allowed. Even so, you were faster than a horse boat, and you could easily overtake. As you pulled up alongside their stern, the suction between the boats put an extra drag on their boat, and the old horse stopped pulling when he found the collar had gone hard. But as you went past, the horse boatman could do the same to you. If he had a mind to touch up his horse when his bow was against your stern, you started pulling him. He could follow you for miles – until he got to a bridge where he had to back off and let you go. If there was a more powerful motor boat behind you, he might want to overtake along the Five Mile Pound, which meant all the locks would be against you going up the Thirty. So you tried to keep going as fast as you could, and some boatmen were known to drop empty crumb sacks or even chicken wire in a bridge hole in the hope it would foul the other boat's propeller.

The usual procedure at a lock was similar to that with a horse boat, but the motor replaced the role of the horse. One of the crew drew the top paddle to stop the boat as it approached the sill, and then he went on to prepare the next lock while the steerer ran up the steps, closed the bottom gates and put the motor in gear slow ahead. When the lock was full, the steerer pushed the top gate open and dropped the paddles, and as the boat moved forward, he jumped aboard. Inevitably things sometimes went wrong, and it was important to be alert for any emergency. One boatman had started to draw the top paddle when he realized his wife had not come up the steps in the usual way. Guessing that she had missed her footing and fallen in the water, he immediately dropped the paddle to stop the flow that could have closed the bottom gates and crushed her. Then he ran back and hurried down the steps to find her in good spirits hanging on to the boat's rudder. Another couple were not so lucky at one of the Stoke Locks. Again the wife fell in, and as the husband went to rescue her, he fell in too and both were drowned.

Another way of working was for one of the crew to keep ahead preparing the locks and leave the steerer to work the boat through on his own. Then when he jumped ashore, he had to run up to draw the top paddle and stop the boat himself before hurrying back to close the bottom gates. While one boatman was working in this way with his wife ahead preparing the next lock, he looked up but couldn't see her. He ran

A Bolinder towing a Petter with the river in flood near Tewkesbury

up to the next lock and still couldn't see her until he realized she had fallen into the chamber. The water was swirling about, but all of a sudden she shot up and he was able to pull her out.

We usually took 8½ to 9 hr from Worcester to Tardebigge, although it could be between 8 and 10 hr according to what cargo we had in. So after 6 hr on the river, we were up somewhere towards Tardebigge that night and into Birmingham by dinner time the next day. There were several stopping places according to where we could get to by the time we were ready to pack up. When it got dark, we used to put a headlight on and go on working until they locked up the locks at about 8 or 9 o'clock. For one special trip, we took a load of sal ammoniac from Gloucester to Birmingham in 22 hr, and a special film was made. The cargo was filmed being unloaded from a ship at Bristol into a motor barge and again at Gloucester when it was trans-shipped to *Motor Boat No. 2*. We had our food all ready, and we went straight through to Birmingham fly, being filmed at Worcester and again going into Birmingham.

Normally you worked steadily to a plan, but if you were in a hurry, you could force the top gate open early. When the water was within a foot or two of the level, the steerer took the boat back and then forward to hit the top gate, and the mate dropped a 4 in square block of oak in to hold it open so that the water came up in no time! This was only done if you were in a hurry to get out of a flight before they locked it or if you wanted to get to a factory to get your trip note in before they closed.

When you had a butty, you could still go almost as fast on the canal as you could go single, but up the locks you had to wait for the butty to be brought up by a horse that was picked up at Worcester and left at Tardebigge. We waited for the butty at the top of the Six, and we pulled them along the Five Mile Pound while they had their meal. The old horse used to have a rest along there, just walking beside the boat, although you might have to shout or throw stones to keep him going. You didn't usually shut the top gate behind you in those days unless you had a butty behind and you wanted to get the lock ready for him. Then, while the motor was going out of the lock, you nipped back and drew half a bottom paddle before getting on board. When the stern passed the top gate, you had the engine running full power and you put

Ex-Cadbury's motor boat *No. 3* towing two butties at Breedon Cross – the lettering was added in the photographer's studio

the rudder hard over to flush the water in behind the gate. This brought it away from the wall, and the pull of the half paddle closed the gate behind you.

The most common places to go were Birmingham and Bournville. General cargoes such as copper, zinc, carbide, sugar and tea went to our own warehouse at Gas Street Basin – you name it, we carried it. Also we did a lot of sugar and chocolate crumb for Cadbury's – Severn and Canal had anything up to twenty-five boats a week from Frampton, and I've seen as many as twenty-one boats at Bournville on a Monday morning waiting to unload. To turn round after discharging there, you had to go on a mile-and-a-half to Selly Oak. We also took wheat to Browns Mill and Watson & Todd in Birmingham. Sometimes we went up to Stourport and on up the Staffordshire and Worcestershire Canal to take wheat to Millers of Wolverhampton or Smiths of Walsall, but this trade was slowing down compared with earlier years. Smiths bought thirty boat loads of wheat at a time from a ship, and they had to have it all. Some boats unloaded at the mill and others at a warehouse at the Pleck, but you still might have to wait three or four days to unload.

We loaded deals at Sharpness, and calcium carbide came out of our barges at Gloucester. We took oil to Butlers next to the timber yard at Gas Street Basin – they had boiled linseed and raw linseed oil there which had come from Foster Brothers at Gloucester. We loaded steel out of the ships at Sharpness, and we took it to Stewarts and Lloyds at Coombeswood [Halesowen] for making tubes. Coming back through Gosty Hill Tunnel, you had to take the range chimney and the engine exhaust right off – you couldn't just lay them down because the top of the boat was only just below the top of the tunnel. The sides of the cabin were almost touching the tunnel, and you could only see ahead by peering over the top of the cabin and keeping your head in the middle.

We never bought any coal for our range – we could always find some if we stopped where there was a coal merchant or at a Cadbury's factory. We carried a rake with a fine mesh gauze, and while we were waiting to unload, we could often rake up a hundredweight out of the canal in no time. Also we had many a piece of large coal as we went past factories like Guest Keen and Nettlefolds. From the engine room, I grabbed a piece that was almost a hundredweight, and my mate at the stern usually got a medium-sized piece as well. We kept the engine going all the time so they didn't think we were stopping, but sometimes they heard the coal rumble and a chap would run out of the boiler house and shout at us! They never put the police on to us though – they used to expect it of the boat people. If gauging then showed you had more on than the consignment note said, the man might comment that you had a load of dunnage on – that's odds and ends. In fact he knew very well how much dunnage you'd really be carrying, so he could guess you had some extra coal on, but he took no notice. We could have been caught millions of times, but all the weighmen used to know us.

From Birmingham, you were sometimes sent to Cadbury's factory at Knighton on the Shropshire Union Canal to collect chocolate crumb and bring it back to Bournville. For several years, Severn and Canal had four horse boats based in Birmingham for this traffic, and the crews lived on their boats fifty-two weeks a year. If they needed more boats, you had to go down to help them out, and some weeks they used over twenty boats.

Coming back to Gloucester, we were more often empty than we were loaded. We might have a load of mass back from Bournville to Frampton or a few empty bags for refilling with chocolate. Occasionally, we might go into Birmingham and bring a load of telephone wire back to be trans-shipped for Germany, or we might go to Littleton Colliery to bring down coal for the tugs. Also sometimes we called at Stoke Prior and loaded salt for the schooners in the New Basin at Gloucester. Coming

Motors and butties at Gas Street Basin, Birmingham

back down to Stourport, you might be lucky and pick up a load of sugar for Frampton. There was a big sugar beet factory at the top of Stour Pound, and the sugar was brought by road for you to pick up in Stourport basin. But there wasn't much down traffic, and usually we came back to Gloucester empty.

Leaving Birmingham at six in the morning, we were at Gloucester that night – 3 hr to Tardebigge, 6½ hr down the canal and 3½ hr down the river. It was quicker coming down the locks than going up because they empty quicker than they fill. It took a bit longer when towing a butty, but we could still get down to Gloucester in a day with a pair of boats. If we left Birmingham in the afternoon and we couldn't get right down the canal before they locked up the locks, we often stopped at Tommy Thompson's – a pub called the Halfway House. Or we went down to see Freddie Teal, a lock-keeper, and we played cards at his house until 2 or 3 o'clock in the morning. Those were the best two pounds on the flight that didn't run empty and leave your boat on the bottom. The lock-keepers had to go up and down in the evening to see the top gates weren't fouled, but a lot of the locks had bad gates and they were half empty next morning. If your pound did run dry, you had to go and drain water all the way down from the summit until you could work through the lock.

Going down a lock, the steerer used a strap to stop the boat and close the gate. He put an 8 yd piece of rope round the bollard on the gate and hung on. In this way, he stopped a 10 ton boat going at 4 or 5 miles an hour in a matter of 2 yd. The gate acted as a brake as it pulled to behind the boat, and that's how we could work the locks so fast. The mate drew the inside paddle and then ran down to get the next lock ready. The steerer ran down the outside of his lock and drew the other paddle, and then he got the stem of his boat between the fork of the gate and had his engine going ahead dead slow. When the lock was empty, he dropped the bottom paddles and pushed open the bottom gates, stepping across from one to the other on the footboards. Then as the boat started to come out of the lock, he jumped down on top of the cabin and revved up the engine.

Some of the boatmen left the engine in neutral while working the lock, and they had a line attached to the clutch lever to start the boat coming out when the gates were open. Normally we left the gates open, but if your butty was coming behind, you shut them to help him along. Meanwhile the mate had been getting the next lock ready, and by the time the boat got there, he was just opening the top gate ready for it to

slide straight in. That's how you kept going all the way down – it was
timed so well that each gate opened before the boat got there.

When my Dad died, I was given special help to get back to Gloucester
quickly. We were unloading the boat at Birmingham, and it was
3 o'clock in the afternoon when the gaffer called me into the office to
give me the news. He knew my Mum would be worried, and so he
arranged for the locks to be left open for me all the way down. When I
came to Tardebigge, there was a lock-keeper on both sides of the gate,
Freddie Teal and Danny Merrill, and they had filled all the locks ready
for me as they'd walked up. They helped me down in record time –
thirty locks in just over an hour. I never went astern once – we put a
strap around the bollard on the gate to stop us in each lock and close the
gate at the same time. I was still strapping after the gate was shut
because the lock-keepers had the bottom paddles open to help pull the
boat in, and I had to stop her hitting the bottom gate. With all the water
gushing through the paddles, the weirs were running ahead of us, and
as they couldn't take it all, by about the ninth lock down the water
flooded over the canal banks! We went down that fast, my hands ended
up smothered in blisters. I was in Worcester in $8\frac{1}{2}$ hr, and I stopped there
overnight. Next morning, I started at 6 o'clock, and I was home in
Gloucester by 10 o'clock.

Unloading spelter at Severn and Canal's Birmingham warehouse with *Motor No.8*
behind

Normally when you got to Worcester, you carried on down the river on your own, but occasionally you might find a boat waiting there, and you towed it down to Gloucester. This didn't happen very often because usually the boatmen had it all mapped out how far they were going to go. But some were a bit lazy, and instead of coming right down the canal for their day, they stopped somewhere and got on the beer. Then they might miss the tug at Worcester, and so you took them down the river if you had plenty of time. When you got back to Gloucester, the motor boats took first turn, even if there were thirty horse boats waiting for a cargo. This caused a big grievance within the company because the horse boatmen could be on the dole and the motor boatmen kept going all the time. But they had to put up with it – that's how it was in those days. There was no argument – the company could say 'You're finished' and give you the brown envelope with your cards in.

When there was a lot of fresh in the river, we could get down to Gloucester very quickly. We came straight out of Danny Watton's top lock, straight over the weirs and we were in Gloucester in 2½ hr, but there were sometimes difficulties with the bridges. Usually we just went under Upton Bridge, but if the river was high, we had to get it swung open. We only had a blower to warn them, and when we were travelling so fast, they couldn't get the bridge open in time, so we had to turn round and head into the stream until they were ready. To know whether I would have headroom at the bridge, I had a mark on the brick wall of a drainage culvert almost 3 miles upstream. One time I was belting towards the bridge at about 12 miles an hour when I realized something was wrong. I must have mistaken my mark by one brick, and I was going to be 3 in too high. We had stripped down the cratch and everything, but the boat used to squat on her backside when she was travelling fast, and I was frightened her bow wouldn't go under. When we got to the bridge, the stud was flattened bang down on to the foredeck, I jumped into the cabin just holding on to the tiller and we swept under the bridge. I was the last to go through that night, and the water level was only about 4 in off stopping the bridge swinging. The next morning, it had risen about another foot and all the traffic was stopped.

When the river was high, we didn't run at Black Bridge or Westgate Bridge near Gloucester – we used to turn round and drop down stern first with the pig dragging along the bottom. Then you could use the rudder to move your stern across, but it didn't move your bow, and as there was a bend in the river, you could be pushed over to the side. So to drop through a bridge, the mate tied the pig rope round the mast beam, and when necessary, he moved it across to the other side to keep the boat going through the middle of the arch. Approaching the bridge, you didn't use the engine – you had to have the pig all but holding her. As soon as you drifted into the bridge hole, the water level dropped 6 in and your stern dropped down. Then you could go full speed astern, dragging your pig down the middle of the river until you were through the bridge.

With the boat empty and the cratch down, the stud on the bow was the highest point, and if necessary the mate used a plank to help squeeze the stud under the bridge. He put the plank up over the bulkhead and rested it on top of the stud, and as we went through the bridge, it knocked the bow down so the stud would go under without catching. One time we had got through the Black Bridge this way, but the water was too high for us to get under Westgate Bridge, so we tied up by a big willow tree at the back of the gypsy camp and we walked home. It was nine days before the lock-keeper thought the water had dropped low enough for us to get through, and when we went back up to the boat, we found it had so much rain water inside that it was half way up the flywheel. It took us an hour to pump out enough to clear the engine, and when we got it going, my mate used the plank again, and down we went under the bridge. By this time, the river was 2 in below the Berkeley Canal and dropping, so the lock-keeper opened the floodgates and let us in.

Nearly all the Severn and Canal boats were in the dock, and they were all loaded over by Gloucester Lock. Although we had only just come in off the river, we were called over straight away to put a load in to go back up to Birmingham. The next morning, the river level was 21 ft 9 in, which meant we could just go back up through the bridge loaded and with the cratch up. There were forty boats all waiting to go away, but none of the other boatmen would move. I offered to give one of them a tow, and the gaffer said we could have the tug *Progress*, but none of them would come. So we went through the lock and started up the river on our own, and all the other boatmen walked up to Westgate Bridge to watch.

We dropped the mast in its box so we'd be as low as possible, and I cleared the water can off the cabin top and took the chimneys down. I told my mate to put the engine down two notches on the bracket so she would run cold for a time, and as we were going up past the top of the Quay, she was blowing out all blue smoke. There was a hell of a current

Motor boat *Oak* at Gas Street Basin

coming through the bridge and I had to go up the middle. Just before the bridge, I told my mate to shove her up five notches to give her more power, and I bet I had over 20 hp out of her for a short period. She was pushing her own deck under water up through that bridge. If I'd gone on like that, the engine would have blown up, so as soon as we were above the bridge, my mate put her back to normal running, and I waved cheerio to the chaps watching!

Two hours later, we were going up over Tewkesbury Weir, and after 6¼ hr, we were going into Danny Watton's top lock. We got up to Stoke Prior that night and went into Birmingham around dinner time the next day. As we started unloading, I was told to go and see the managing director. I thought I must have done something wrong, but he just wanted to know if I had any trouble getting up the river and why the other men wouldn't come. I said the timing showed we had no trouble, but the other men were frightened, and he gave me a bonus of 5s. We got back to Blackpole before meeting the first of the other boats coming up the canal, and we were back in Gloucester before they all had left.

# CHAPTER 10

# Severn Motor Barges and Tankers

*As part of George Cadbury's plan to develop fresh sources of traffic, the Severn and Canal Carrying Company ordered a new type of Severn motor barge from Charles Hill and Sons of Bristol. It was designed to be sufficiently seaworthy to go down to Avonmouth and across to Swansea, but it was small enough just to pass through the locks between Worcester and Stourport.*

The first of the new motor barges, Severn Trader, was built in 1932 and her maiden voyage proved to be quite eventful. Having collected her from Hill's yard, we loaded 160 tons of copper at Bristol, and as we were coming down the Bristol river on the ebb tide, we ran into fog. It was so bad that the skipper in the wheel-box couldn't see past the bow, so two of us went forward as lookouts. When we could see something through the fog, we shouted out 'Port a bit' or 'Starboard a bit' and in this way we eventually got to Avonmouth, where we moored for the night in the Drain [the Old Entrance]. It had cleared up by next morning, but we had only just got out of the Drain when down came the fog again and we couldn't see where we were. We should have been heading across to the Welsh side, but after a time I spotted something in the water which turned out to be the Northwick buoy on the English side. It was a wonder we hadn't hit the bottom. The skipper set a course to get back into the main channel, but it was raining by then and we still couldn't see anything. After a time, the rain cleared off allowing us to see the Chapel Light, and from there we made our way up to Sharpness.

Coming up the canal, the skipper had a devil of a job to get her through all the bridges. She was very slow steering – he moved the wheel over one way, and once she started to turn, he couldn't get the

146

wheel back fast enough before she was turning the other way. Approaching a bridge, he often had to let her run into the bank rather than try to pull her round and risk hitting the brickwork. She was a terror – it took us 5 hr to get up the canal. When we got to Gloucester a lot of bargemen and boatmen were waiting for us, but the skipper couldn't control her, and she came stem on into the corner of the Old Arm. Fortunately we weren't coming fast, and there wasn't much damage. After that, she had to go back to Hills to have the gearing altered a bit. Even then she was slow to respond, and later they put on a bigger wheel and a longer quadrant so it would move the rudder a bit faster.

*Severn Trader* had a three cylinder Kromhout engine. To start it, you put the blowlamps on, and when it was warm enough, you turned on the compressed air and pulled the starting handle. You had to have the fly-wheel in just the right place or otherwise it started going the wrong way. When this happened, we left it running backwards for a time to pump up the air bottles again, and then we stopped it and tried starting again. On one of the sister vessels, *Severn Transport*, the fly-wheel came

*Severn Trader* discharging to a longboat at Gloucester

undone a bit while running backwards like this, and it messed the shaft up. Once started, the engine was controlled from the wheelhouse, so you didn't have to have a man down below. On the later barges, *Severn Industry* had a Petter engine, where we used to put in little cartridges to get it going, and *Severn Merchant* had a Ruston and Hornsby engine. The skipper's quarters were on one side of the engine, and the crew's quarters with two bunks and a range for cooking were on the other side.

The motor barges often towed one or two dumb barges like *Wye*, *Severn, Lillia Venn, Nelson* and *Togo*, and going down the canal we might also take some longboats to Frampton or Sharpness. There was a bridgeman at each bridge to open one side and a passman on a push bike opened the other side. Approaching a bridge, you'd blow for the bridgeman, and he was usually out in time to open up so you could go straight through. But if you did have to stop for some unforeseen reason and you were towing a dumb barge, the barge came up behind you, and you had to put a short rope on and go astern with the barge close to. Or if there was a soft bank, you let the barge slide along the bank a bit to stop her that way.

Going down to Avonmouth, you could lock in on a big tide, but at neap tides you had to moor in the Drain and go in with the first locking of the next tide. We usually met the ships and loaded out of them directly with the dockers stowing the cargo. You were lucky to load the same day you docked as often what you wanted was at the bottom of the ship, and you had to wait for them to get down to it. The Severn motor barges could carry up to 160 tons – wheat, copper, steel, spelter, carbide, fruit, cocoa beans, sugar and a lot of Typhoo tea in cases. Most times you had just one commodity, but sometimes you had mixed cargoes. To get a good load of cocoa beans on, we filled the hold up, put the hatches on and then put three or four hundred sacks on the top, but we had to leave a bit of space near the mast to get our boat on board. Sometimes we went on up to Bristol to load from the Bristol City ships, the Navigation ships [Bristol Steam], the Stroom ships [Holland Steam] or the Coast ships.

Normally we locked out of Avonmouth through the New Entrance, but occasionally this was blocked by a banana boat taking on passengers. Between tides, they lowered the lock a bit so the passengers could walk straight on, and then they were ready to go out when the tide came in. When this happened, we had to go through the junction and come out of the Old Entrance. Often we went out on a night tide and came up to Sharpness by about 2 or 3 o'clock in the morning. We went up as far as Purton Bridge, and we waited there until morning when the passman arrived to bring us on up to Gloucester, opening and closing all the bridges for us.

In the early days, most of the loads were trans-shipped into longboats at Gloucester using the electric crane there as well as our own gear. If they wanted the motor barge back down for another cargo quickly, you discharged at Gloucester and let the longboats take it up to Birmingham. Once we did two trips between Avonmouth and Gloucester in a week, loading two boats at a time at Gloucester – one each side. For working our derrick, we had one man on the winch, the skipper on the deck and the mate down in the hold with someone else helping him. The motor for the winch was started with a cartridge – you had some stuff like blotting paper that you rolled up to the thickness of a pencil. You lit it, put it in the hole and put the compression cap on. Then you wound the handle and away she went. The winch was controlled by a clutch, but it often gave trouble. You pushed it in to start the hoist working, and then it wouldn't come out. Whatever you were picking up went right up to the top of the derrick until the jolt of hitting the block made it drop

*Severn Merchant* and longboats in the Old Arm at Gloucester

down. I'd shout 'Look out' to the chap in the hold, and he soon got to know what I meant, although I always managed to stop it by the foot brake. For working with the crane at Gloucester, there was another gang of men in the hold, and the cargo was soon unloaded.

Sometimes we went up to Worcester and unloaded into lorries just above Worcester Bridge on the St John's side where there was a low part of the quay. If we were towing a dumb barge, that tied up on the outside and we used our derrick to empty both. More often, we went right up to Stourport, where we also had to use our own gear in the early days. The first time we went to Stourport, we took a thousand sacks of wheat for transfer into four longboats to go on to Smiths Mill at Walsall. We stopped at Upton upon Severn on the Thursday night and went on to Stourport in the morning. It snowed all day Friday, and the men wouldn't work in the snow, so we just had to wait. On Saturday, it was raining, but we did the unloading, and it was finished about 7 o'clock in the evening. With all the rain after the snow, by Sunday morning the river level was rising fast. The skipper didn't know much about the Severn, but I'd been up and down there for years, and I told him we had to get going. We left at 7 o'clock on Sunday morning and we were down in Gloucester by lunch time, but we only just made it through Westgate Bridge. I told the skipper to get the wheel-box down, we lowered the funnel and the mast so everything was level with the hatch coaming and even the toilet cover flopped over. I told the skipper how to steer through the bridge, but there wasn't much room to spare and he nearly had a child! 'Don't you dare do that' he said. 'Too late, Skipper' I replied. 'We've done it.' The boss gave me 10s for helping the skipper – we wouldn't have got through the bridges otherwise.

Later Severn and Canal developed a site known as Redstone Wharf just below Stourport, where they had a steam crane on a wooden jetty. Most of the cargoes went directly on to lorries or down into a compound where metals could be stored out in the open. We took a lot of spelter and steel to Stourport. We liked a load of steel because the long lengths could be discharged so easily. During loading, pieces of dunnage about 2 or 3 in square had been put between layers of steel and this allowed the sling chains to slide underneath. When it came to unloading, all you had to do was put chains round the steel again, and it was lifted out by the crane 2 tons at a time. Occasionally we loaded wheat into longboats using our own derrick. The boats were stopped there on their way back from a previous trip, but they didn't mind because down at Gloucester, there could have been twenty or thirty boats in front of them, whereas

*Severn Trader* and other vessels at Redstone Wharf Stourport

by turning round at Stourport they were jumping the queue. Once the boats were loaded, a tug had to tow them up to the locks at the entrance to the Staffordshire and Worcestershire Canal. After discharging, we just let go the bow rope, and the current swung the barge round on the stern rope. Then we slackened the rope, and the man on the wharf chucked it off the mooring post.

Although the most common port for loading was Avonmouth, we also had many trips to Bristol and the South Wales ports. When going to Newport, we couldn't leave Sharpness and be down in time to get into the lock on the same tide, but we had enough water to get into Newport river and we dropped anchor there. When coming back from Bristol, Cardiff or Newport, we couldn't get up the river or into Avonmouth on that tide. Most times, we went into the Old Entrance at Avonmouth and tied alongside the pier, but this dried out at low tide, and if we couldn't get in there, we anchored in the bay by the mouth of the Avon off Portishead. We picked up timber off the ships at Cardiff and took it to Stourport. We went to the Roath Dock at Cardiff and picked up bulk wheat from Spillers that we brought up to Reynolds at Gloucester or Healings at Tewkesbury. The wheat was sucked out of the hold, and we had to go down and shovel it near to the sucker. The worst cargo was when we had fetch coal from Newport and take it up to the top of Gloucester Quay for the steam tugs. To unload, we had to shovel it into skips which were lifted out on the derrick. We spent all day emptying it, and then we had to give the hold a good scrub out afterwards.

As well as the new barges for dry cargoes, there was a big increase in the number of tanker barges carrying petroleum products during the 1930s. The earliest tanker barges on the river were *Shell Mex 7* and the two we called 'Black Bats', *Loyaltie* and *Sinceritie*, and these were towed everywhere by tugs. In the early days, the Severn Commission wouldn't allow a steam tug in the same lock as a tanker because of concern about a spark from the funnel. It was all right for a motor tug to be in a lock with a tanker, but they were not allowed a fire in the cabin stove. Then John Harker from Knottingley introduced small motor tankers paired with dumb barges, and Severn and Canal decided to try the same.

The dumb barge *Severn Carrier II* was ready first, and we took her straight from Charles Hill's yard to Avonmouth and picked up 80 tons of

*Severn Carrier*

petrol. She could carry nearly 200 tons when full, but it was a trial run to see how she fitted in the small locks above Worcester. We got to Stourport all right, and this was the very first cargo that Regent put into their tanks there. But when we started to come back down through Lincomb Lock, we couldn't work it as the rudder caught on the sill. We had to fill the lock again and go back up. The tug had to lock back up as well, pull us out and turn us round so we could come down stern first – that was the only way we could get through. When we got down to Gloucester, they put shackles on each side of the rudder so you could disconnect it and turn it sideways. They also added a piece under the stern of the barge to make it a balanced rudder. When the motor barge *Severn Carrier* came, she usually pulled *Carrier II*. At that time, we had no heating on *Carrier II* – they just supplied us with duffel coats to sleep in. If you wanted a cup of tea, they made a pot on *Carrier* and sent it back to us on a line! What we put up with in those days, but work was so scarce, you were only too glad of anything.

Later in the 1930s, Severn and Canal had four more motor tankers built by Charles Hill and Sons at Bristol, *Severn Traveller*, *Severn Tanker*, *Severn Rover* and *Severn Voyager*, and the company took over four of the dumb barges that were already on the river. Then *Carrier II* was towed by any motor barge that was available, but she was difficult to handle as she was a very fast boat and awkward to steer. One time, she ran past her motor barge as it was slowing down, and the rope got tangled round a ventilator. Unfortunately, the rope also went round a chap's stomach and it killed him. After that, a lot of motor barge skippers refused to tow her, and they usually put her with one of the small motor tugs – *Carrier II* and *Enterprise* would just fit into Gloucester Lock.

The early Harkers motor barges included *Janet*, *John Harker*, *Tiger* and *Cynthia*, and these were followed by *Limnell*, *Nancy* and *Victor*. Each usually towed a dumb barge. Most of the crews were Yorkshiremen who lived on the barges and only went home occasionally, and there was great rivalry between them and the Severn and Canal crews. Both firms paid low weekly wages with extra money for each trip, and Harkers were always trying to pinch your turn so they could load or discharge first. By the end of the 1930s, there were three more pairs of barges on the river run by the Regent Petroleum Company: *Regent Jill* towed *Regent Jack*, *Regent Lady* towed *Regent Lord* and *Regent Queen* towed *Regent King*. *Regent Jack* and *Regent Lord* were very awkward barges – towing them was like pulling a row of houses along!

The crew on a motor barge was two men and a boy, and just two men on a dummy. We usually did about two trips a week or almost three when there were long evenings. Leaving Gloucester on a Sunday, we locked into Avonmouth early Monday morning, we loaded all day Monday, came up to Sharpness that night and up the canal on Tuesday morning. Then we went up to Worcester or Stourport to discharge, and we came down on Wednesday ready to do the whole thing again in the next three days. You grabbed an hour or two of sleep now and again on your run. You were at Avonmouth for a few hours, and then you could all get your heads down, but otherwise you had to sleep when you could – one at a time. We had no social life at all. If you had a chance of getting home, you were too tired to go out and you were only too glad to get into bed.

Going to Avonmouth, you made sure you left Gloucester in plenty of time to catch the tide at Sharpness. They were not supposed to let you out of Sharpness more than a quarter of an hour before high water, but I've gone out an hour before! If you were early, you sneaked up to the corner of the pier and, as the barge hit the tide, you opened up the engine and pushed into it. You could be there for ten minutes or more before starting to make a track. You went on down to the point and past the buoys, and then you got across towards Chepstow, down to Severn Tunnel and across to Avonmouth. A tanker went down one day in a thick fog and he went aground near Charston Rock. He had a *Cleprod* tanker barge on behind, and fortunately this came down past him, set the rope up and pulled him off. As he squared up, the fog cleared and suddenly he could see Avonmouth across the other side of the estuary. Usually you got into Avonmouth on the same tide, but a slow boat might have to tie up on the pier outside the New Entrance.

Inside Avonmouth, you'd bear left, and the oil dock was right up the top on the left. There was a boom across in case there was a leak of oil, and they had to open this for you to go in alongside one of the jetties. At the jetty, you connected the pipes and controlled the valves while the jetty-man worked the pumps. You loaded the stern tank so much and then the other tanks, so she came down on an even keel, and then you adjusted the trim by opening valves to allow flow from one tank to another. Some tankers ended up loaded 6 in by the head, some were better on a level keel and others were better a couple of inches down at the stern.

When it was time to leave, they opened the boom, and it was like a madhouse with everyone trying to get into the lock first. There was room for three abreast in the lock, and the best position was in the middle, because when the gates were opening, the middle boat could get out first. Then you were all off round the pier as fast as you could go to try and get to Sharpness first. The first into Sharpness lock would be the first up the canal, and the first to lock out into the river again at Gloucester. You were supposed to follow the channel but we all took short cuts if we could. It was a proper cut-throat job because you were all after the first lock at Sharpness and only six barges could fit in. It seemed some of the skippers just had to keep moving – they'd tear up to Sharpness before the tide was up if they could, and we always said they should have wheels some of them. You got to Sharpness before high tide, and you had to be careful not to get carried past, because the channel narrowed and the tide became a lot stronger.

Approaching Sharpness, you turned round to face into the tide, and you waited for the signal to go into the dock. When the lock was clear, the first boat turned in, and the others followed in turn. If it was a big tide, you daren't go up too far or if something happened, you'd be under the Severn Railway Bridge before you could do anything about it – the tide does rush up past there. So you turned round by the swinging light, and you hung about there until the tide slackened. When you judged it was right, you let the tide take you gradually backwards

Tanker barges entering Sharpness Lock

towards the entrance, but you had to have a reliable engine to punch against the tide and hold you where you wanted to be. You aimed to get to the piers as the lock was ready and then you could turn in. Some boats got in behind the second pier, especially if they were towing a dumb barge. Then as the tide slackened, they tried the strength of it until they found they could get out.

This turning operation was more tricky if you were towing a dumb barge, and the consequences of things going wrong could be very serious. On the night of 4 February 1939, I was bringing *Severn Traveller* up from Avonmouth, helping to tow *Severn Carrier* and *Severn Pioneer*. It was a big spring tide, and we turned round before Sharpness and dropped up stern first to be ready to come in when the signal went clear. Then the boy came to me and said 'This rope's all slack skipper.' I knew there was something wrong, and I told him to pull the rope in. *Carrier* was not sufficiently powerful to hold *Pioneer* against the tide, and both were being swept round by the old entrance to Sharpness, so I turned *Traveller* round to go and help. We got a rope aboard them again, but by that time we were close to the Severn Railway Bridge, and with the tide rushing past the piers, there was a big drop in water level. *Pioneer* hit the bridge, *Carrier* hit the bridge and turned over, and we were swept over her keel. Then *Traveller* hit the bridge and went over on one side before righting herself again. My engineer was thrown into the water, but he managed to grab one of the life chains and I helped him back on board. The blades on *Traveller's* propeller were sheared off in the incident, and so all we could do was drop the anchor and wait. Eventually a small boat came and rescued us, but the other crewmen were all drowned.

Whoever was first in the lock at Sharpness was first up the canal, and the others followed in their turn. If you came into Sharpness in the evening, you had to go out of the docks because you had petrol in, but you couldn't go through Purton bridge because there was no bridgeman on duty. The first motor barge put his dummy alongside the bank and tied up on the outside, and the other pairs tied up behind in the same way. Then most of the crews went up to the Sharpness Hotel for a drink and a game of cards – Shoot they called it. In the morning, you were all supposed to go up the canal in your turn, but there could be some pushing when the bridge opened as the first up the canal would be the first discharging at Worcester. If the first crew overslept, the next wouldn't start their engine as it could wake the others up – instead they'd use a rope quietly to get their barge alongside the first, and then they'd start their engine and go through the bridge first. One crew even

got out in the night, crept across the other barges in their stockinged feet
and lowered the anchors down so they couldn't get away quickly!
Sometimes a motor barge towed two dumb barges up the canal but, if it
was after time, the bridgemen created because they were paid extra for
each pass, and if the boats were roped together it only counted as one
pass. At Gloucester, one of the dumb barges was dropped off and a tug
took it up the Severn.

Coming up on a night tide, you got to Gloucester during the morning,
and you carried on up the river, but if you reached Gloucester in the
afternoon, you liked to go home for the night. You couldn't stop in the
main docks with petrol – you had to go into Monk Meadow Dock which
was kept specially for tankers. In the morning, Gloucester Lock
normally opened at 6 o'clock, but a tanker could order the lock at
5 o'clock if they paid for that extra hour of overtime. Then they were
first through because they were paying, and the other tankers went
through afterwards in their turn. As another way of getting an early
start, some of the tankers locked-out into the river in the afternoon and
tied up on the Quay wall, but they were stopped from doing that
because of the risk of passers-by dropping a match and setting off the
petrol. You could go up above the Black Bridge and tie against the bank
there, but somebody had to stay on board because you were responsible
if anything happened. When you moored in Monk Meadow Dock, you
could all go home because there were two watchmen on duty there.

In the morning, only one pair of tankers could go in the lock at a time
and the others had to wait their turn. Each locking took twenty minutes,
so the last pair might have to wait an hour or two before starting up the
river. As you were going out of the lock, if there was any fresh water in
the river, the current could catch the bow and take the barge across the
channel going down towards the weir. So one of the crew went ashore
with a heaving line, and if necessary he pulled a rope over and put it on
a bollard. Then you picked him up half way along the Quay – he came
down the steps by the Ship Inn and jumped aboard as the barge went by.

Normally you couldn't overtake on the river because the pair from the
previous locking were too far in front, but if there was a drop of fresh
water in the river so the lock didn't have so far to fall and rise, they
might only be ten minutes ahead, and a powerful boat could catch up.
The first pair would go round the inside of a bend to keep out of the
current and if you had a bit more power, you could get up alongside
before the next bend and stop them going over the other side of the river
to get in the slack water there. But if the river wasn't very wide, when

you got alongside the dummy barge, the suction could pull that barge against yours, and you couldn't get by him unless you had a lot of extra power to do it. Then you might come to a shallow part on your side, and you had to ease down because he wouldn't move over to let you by.

At Worcester, the tankers went into the small dock off the river just above Diglis Locks which had previously been used mainly for timber. You coupled up the pipes to discharge, using the boat's pumps or those on shore. One of the crew had to be there all the time watching, but the others could go shopping or get some sleep – we used to take it in turns. In the early days, the Severn Commission wouldn't allow you to connect up or disconnect in the dark. You could carry on discharging provided you had connected up in daylight, but once darkness came, you couldn't disconnect so you had to stay there. Later they put up some lights for people to see where they were walking, and it lit up all the depot as well. Then we could also work at night, and as soon as the tanks were empty, off came the pipes and you were back in the lock and on your way down the river again.

Some of the barges went farther up the river to discharge at wharves near Stourport. All the Severn and Canal barges were made just to fit Lincomb Lock which is the smallest on the river, and you always kept an eye open to see there was no timber in there or you could get jammed. Also silt caused a problem when the water level was very low. The lock was so shallow, you sometimes had to force the barge over the silt in the bottom, and it built up in front of the bow. Even with the engine full speed ahead, you'd be only just moving into the lock and it seemed to take hours to force yourself in. We had so much trouble at one time that the firm told us to reduce our usual draft by 2 in.

Having discharged at Stourport, you usually started straight back down the river, but one time we took *Severn Traveller* for a run up to Bewdley to see if it could be done. We touched bottom several times, but eventually we made it safely, and the firm never found out or we would have been sacked. A later skipper on *Traveller* always had his dog on board, and one day the dog's tail became caught in the chain connecting the wheel to the rudder. To release it, the skipper had to turn the wheel, and this made *Traveller* swing into the bank, but at least the dog's tail was saved!

If there was a lot of water in the river, you had to take the wheel-house down to get under the fixed bridges, but it also meant you got home quickly. One time we came all the way from Stourport to Gloucester without going through a lock – we came over all the weirs.

*Severn Carrier* being filled with water to get under Worcester Bridge

We had to stop at Worcester because of the low bridge, and the fire brigade came and pumped water into the tanks so we could get on down to Gloucester. When the river was really high, to get through Black Bridge and Westgate Bridge you had to turn round and drop down backwards – especially with *Carrier II* because she was such a high thing. In the early days, you had to turn round in the Long Reach above the Tar Works, and the tug left you to manage how you could. The firm sent up a couple of blokes, one each side of the river, and you passed them a line each side. They put it on a post or round a tree or something to check the boat, and we dropped down through the bridges stern first. Hours and hours we used to spend with a rope each side until we complained so much that the firm arranged to dig out a bit of the bank about 500 yd above the Black Bridge. Then the smaller barges could come down and turn round there, although the big ones still had to turn in the Long Reach.

If necessary, the tankers tied up above the Black Bridge and were filled with water before dropping down through the bridges and turning

*Rosa H* stuck under Westgate Bridge

again at the Quay. Motor and dumb barges usually worked together in pairs, but there was one time when the motor barge *Janet* dropped through the bridges first, leaving the crew of the dumb barge *Rosa* to manage on their own. They started drifting backwards dragging their anchor like the pig, but as they were going through Westgate Bridge, the barge fell away to the lower part of the arch and got jammed there. Some of us heard talk of her being stuck, and so we went along to help. We fixed a block in the ground and set up a double rope between the barge and the shore, and four of us started pulling. Gradually we pulled her across to the middle of the arch and, once she was clear, we let her go to drift on down to the Quay.

# CHAPTER 11

# *War and Nationalization*

*In the late 1930s, the Severn and Canal Carrying Company provided an efficient and competitive service to Midlands traders and, when war broke out, the company was able to make an important contribution to the national effort. Because of intensive bombing of London, shipping was diverted to west coast ports, and emergency arrangements were set up to distribute the imports as quickly as possible. Severn and Canal was responsible for carrying thousands of tons of vital cargoes such as metals needed for making weapons, food for the population of the Midlands and petrol for military and civilian use. Tanker barges belonging to John Harker and Regent also carried petroleum products to Gloucester, Worcester and Stourport, and Healings barges regularly took wheat to Tewkesbury.*

Soon after war broke out, Severn and Canal longboats found themselves moving outside their normal runs to carry essential cargoes and these longer journeys brought new experiences. One boat went to Manchester to pick up batteries and, after working down Audlem Locks early one morning, the skipper was about to turn off at Barbridge when he said 'Hey look – there's a ghost on the tow-path!' A man had come out of his house in a nightgown and a long nightcap, and he was waving and shouting 'Stop! Stop!' The Severn and Canal men didn't know that there was a chain across the canal to stop boats going through, and they just broke it and carried on. Later they came to a tunnel where they found a tug that had wheels on either side to rub along the walls when towing horse boats through the tunnel.

The winter of 1939–40 was particularly severe, and boats were frozen-up all over the country. Two motor boats and one horse boat had been told to take sulphate to Ellesmere Port where they picked up sugar. On the way back they became trapped in the ice at Barbridge, and the snow was blocking the tow-path. They soon ran out of food and money, and initially they had to rely on a publican who kept them fed in return for a pledge on their horse. But with no sign of the frost ending, special arrangements were later made for them to sign on the dole, although this meant walking 4 miles into Nantwich and 4 miles back twice a week. They were stuck there for six weeks until the thaw came.

None of the Severn and Canal boats were damaged by enemy action, but traffic was slightly disrupted as a result of the bombing in the Birmingham area. In October 1940, three bombs fell on Worcester Wharf, beside Gas Street Basin, partly destroying the premises of T.J. Graham & Sons. Six weeks later, there was a direct hit on the Bournville Lane aqueduct which was badly damaged, causing the canal water to escape into Bournville Lane. The canal was closed to traffic for twelve weeks while repairs were carried out, and boats for Birmingham were diverted up the Staffordshire and Worcestershire and Stourbridge Canals. This unusual traffic upset a lock-keeper's wife on the Stourbridge Canal – late one evening she heard a Petter diesel approaching, and she came running out of her house thinking it was an enemy plane.

A more important effect on the operation of the longboats was the

Boats left high and dry at Cadbury's warehouse following bomb damage to Bournville Lane aqueduct in 1940

difficulty of getting crews. Even before the war, quite a number of boatmen had transferred to the growing number of tankers coming on the Severn and, with the outbreak of war, matters became worse because some of the men were called up for active service. All sorts of replacements were tried, including ne'er-do-wells, but few were any good because they were not brought up to it. Later on, three women volunteers were given some training with the help of the author of *Idle Women*. They tried out a horse boat on the Gloucester and Sharpness Canal just above Hempsted Bridge where they would not cause any disturbance. The ground behind there was being used as a prisoner of war camp, and the prisoners all came out to see this boat being pulled up and down. But when the women set their horse up to pull, the line broke because it was old and they were left drifting. They knotted it together, but as soon as the horse took up the weight it broke again. There were one or two things that went wrong like that, and the volunteers only did a few trips.

To help keep the boats working, the government sent some soldiers down and two were put on a longboat. The tugmen got them to Worcester and told them what to do, and then they were on their own. They picked up a horse and away they went up the Worcester and Birmingham Canal, but they soon had problems. They got jammed in the King's Head Lock which is the narrowest lock on the canal – if there was only a stick in there, it could jam a longboat. Then near the top of Lowesmoor Pound, they must have gone too close to the tow-path, as a stone got underneath their rudder and lifted it off. The boat ran ashore, but the horse was still trying to pull until eventually one soldier realized that he had to shout 'Whoa!' After some discussion about how they were going to get the rudder back on, they both jumped in the canal and stood in the water trying to lift the rudder, but they couldn't manage to fit it into place. Fortunately, there was a boatman coming up behind them, and he had a good laugh as there is a special way of doing it. He stood straddle-legged across the hatches, lifted the tiller between his legs and dropped the rudder back into place, watched by the soldiers who were still in the canal.

Meanwhile, the barge traffic through Gloucester was recognized as being very important, particularly with all the petroleum tankers bringing vital supplies to the Midlands, and something had to be done to prevent the hold-ups that occurred at Westgate Bridge when the river level was high. In 1941, therefore, the carriageway of the bridge was replaced by a steel girder structure at a higher level, and preparations were made to demolish the stone arch that had been such a problem to boatmen over the years. The plan was to blow out the keystone with explosive and, to prevent the stones then falling into the river, each was suspended by a wire from the girders above. But when the charges were fired, every wire broke and all the stones fell into the river. It took three days to clear enough of the channel to get vessels through, and the dredger was kept busy for some time before it was all clear. This operation removed the worst source of delay, but there could still be occasional hold-ups at the Black Bridge, just upstream, until it too was replaced after the war.

To handle the growing barge traffic from Avonmouth, two tugs were used on each tide to keep everything moving – one tug came up with a tow while another was locking out of Sharpness. The tug coming up brought its tow into the dock and usually waited to go down on the next tide. They limited the number of barges to four, so the tug going down could usually get straight into the New Entrance at Avonmouth on the same tide. In this way, the barges were loaded and back out again on the next tide. Sometimes one of the motor tankers helped with the tow down to Avonmouth. There was no point in them racing, because the tug had to go in the same lock, and so it saved them time to help the tug along.

This regular pattern was sometimes disrupted, however, as there was a lot of bombing at Avonmouth. One particular night, the tug *Primrose* was waiting to go in to the dock when a bomb dropped close under her stern. Another time the tug was tied up by the entrance lock, and a bomb dropped in the dry dock practically alongside. Sometimes the tug couldn't get into the dock because of the bombing, and then they took the barges and ran up on the mud between Avonmouth and Portishead. When the crew got up one morning, they found shrapnel on the deck from the guns firing at the bombers. Another night the tug went down from Sharpness, and Avonmouth was on fire. The bombers had hit the petrol tanks and the tug crew thought they'd never see the place again. They went on down to Walton Bay, anchored there for the night and returned to Avonmouth the next morning. They found the old pier was burnt down, and the Old Entrance was not used much after that. While all this was happening, the dock authorities stopped the tugs going straight into Avonmouth because they didn't like the gates being open for long. They had a submarine net across the entrance which had to be lowered when the gates were open, and they wanted to get all vessels in and out quickly near to high tide so they could get the net fixed again.

Then the tug had to go from Sharpness to Slime Road and lie on the mud there so it could get to Avonmouth early on the next tide. This did slow the traffic down, but they had to do it for a time.

Minesweepers were used in the Bristol Channel below Avonmouth, but they didn't sweep the estuary up to Sharpness so the tugs had to take pot luck. This danger was highlighted when *Severn Transport* hit a mine in an area that was supposed to have been swept. She was going to Cardiff to pick up a load of steel for Stourport, and as she passed between the Welsh Grounds Lightship and the Monkstone Lighthouse, there was an enormous explosion. Two of the crew scrambled out on deck to find there was water rushing into the hold through a hole in the starboard side, part of the wheelhouse was blown away and the skipper was on his knees with both his ankles broken. The engineer was trapped in the engine-room as a tank had moved across to block the hatchway, but the fourth hand managed to squeeze past the tank and helped to get him out. Three parts of the hatches had been blown off, and the lifeboat on them had got jammed between the rails and the hatch coaming. The crew used some of the remaining planks to lever it over into the water and they all got into it, although it was badly holed and only the air tanks were keeping it afloat. As they drifted away, they saw *Transport* go down stern first. An RAF launch came looking for them but couldn't see them because the sea was choppy and they were so low in the water. They continued drifting down between Flat Holm and Steep Holm until eventually a plane spotted them, and then they were picked up by a minesweeper and taken to Barry.

As the war continued, a lot of big ships came to Avonmouth, many from America, and the dock was chock-a-block at times. Everything you could think of came on these ships, from railway engines to live chickens in pens on top of the hatches. Severn and Canal took on the responsiblity of handling frozen meat coming into Avonmouth instead of London. Some insulated barges were brought round from the Thames, and the motor tug *Enterprise* was based at Avonmouth for a time to move these around. The meat had to be discharged from the ship quickly, so it went first into the barges, and when the ship had gone, the cranes were available to put the meat ashore for transport to the cold stores.

To help the distribution of imports, a Bristol Channel Barge Pool was set up under the jurisdiction of the Ministry of War Transport. The pool had control of all the dry cargo barges capable of trading between Avonmouth and Sharpness, including twenty-eight normally centred on Gloucester and twelve on Bristol. Most of the barges went through to Redstone Wharf at Stourport with final delivery of the cargo being carried out by lorry. Trans-shipment into longboats at Gloucester declined due to the difficulty of getting crews, and many boats were sold to firms carrying coal to the Midlands power stations. Recognizing this trend, Severn and Canal changed its name to the Severn Carrying Company in 1942, although inland canal traffic did continue for several more years.

To speed the turn-round of dry cargo barges at Stourport, a new 180 ft long wharf was constructed by the Ministry of War Transport just below Redstone Wharf. It was named Nelson Wharf after the head of the Inland Waterways Division of that Ministry, and it was opened on Trafalgar Day in 1942. It had a large transit shed which was needed to handle the bigger movements that were coming along because the ships arrived at Avonmouth in convoys. The Bristol Channel Barge Pool had control of all the general cargo barges, and the Severn Carrying Company had the responsibility up the river to get the barges unloaded and back quickly. All sorts of special arrangements had to be made, and there was very close liaison between everyone involved. There was also a Severn Tanker Barge Pool which arranged the delivery of petroleum products to existing depots and to new underground storage sites near Gloucester, Upton and Stourport.

During 1944, the barges carried cargoes down-river from Nelson Wharf as part of the preparations for the D-Day invasion of Europe. Hundreds of tons of electrical equipment were taken down to Gloucester, and a firm in Birmingham sent thousands of petrol cans which were taken on to Avonmouth to be loaded on the ships that were going out to the troops. In the same year, Diglis Wharf and transit shed were built beside the river at Worcester, providing space for three barges to be loaded or discharged simultaneously. Also, six new dumb barges called *Sabrinas*, were built by Charles Hill and Sons at Bristol for the Ministry of War Transport, and these were operated as part of the Severn Carrying Company fleet. By the end of the war, the Severn Carrying Company had been responsible for handling over one million tons of cargo of all kinds, including 592,000 tons of petroleum and fuel oil, 131,000 tons of metals, 74,000 tons of wheat and flour, 43,000 tons of butter and cheese, 34,000 tons of canned food and 87,000 tons of other foodstuffs.

After the war, Severn Carrying Company tugs and barges took part in several water carnivals at Worcester and Stourport, and a lot of effort went into the planning of these events. One year at Worcester, *Enterprise*

Longboats being towed up river viewed from Mythe Bridge. Note the new company name on the cloths

*Severn Merchant* passing Nelson Wharf below Stourport

towed a barge that had four masts set up with garlands of flowers and lights, and the bargemen were dressed up as though they were crossing the Equator. In half of the barge, they had a big tarpaulin wedged all round and filled with water and, of course, someone got thrown in. On another barge, there were a lot of fireworks, and a man on board was supposed to set the fireworks going when they got above Worcester Bridge. But he was so drunk that he put a light inside the box and everything blew up with one big bang!

Another year at Stourport, *Enterprise* was fitted up with a perforated pipe connected to a pump in the engine room so that it was spraying water up over the stern. Hidden under the woodwork were red green and yellow lights, shining on the fountain so it looked like a peacock's tail. The skipper's daughter was sitting on top of the wheel-house in the middle of a big gold and silver paper star. From above it looked lovely and, as they went under Stourport Bridge, everybody started dropping money, but unfortunately some of it hit the little girl on the head.

With the return of peacetime conditions, the Severn Carrying Company issued a publicity leaflet, which highlighted its long history and emphasized the excellent service offered by the company's specially

Motor tug *Enterprise* decorated for Stourport Carnival

designed motor barges. The leaflet stated that goods could reach
Stourport from Avonmouth in about 24 hr and pointed out that 2½ million
people lived within 25 miles of Stourport. Cheap overside delivery
reduced the total transit costs and minimized the risk of damage and
pilferage, which resulted in low insurance premiums on goods in
transit. Commodities regularly handled in large quantities included
steel, alumimium, copper, lead, calcium carbide, timber, sugar,
chemicals, foodstuffs, cocoa beans and liquids in bulk. Diglis Wharf and
transit shed at Worcester had handling facilities which included diesel
cranes of 2- and 5-ton capacity and a suction plant and conveyor for bulk
handling of grain. Nelson Wharf and transit shed at Stourport also had
two mobile cranes and a number of trucks, conveyors and weighing
machines etc. The leaflet referred to subsequent distribution by road
vehicles, and no mention was made of any motor boats using the
narrow canals although some still did.

Immediately after the war, the company was able to declare modest
dividends, but during 1947 the directors found that they were trading at
a loss. As government control was due to end, more competition could
be expected from the railways and so there was real concern about the
future. The canals were being brought under the control of the new
British Transport Commission and, to safeguard the interests of shareholders and staff, the directors decided to approach the Commission to
see if they would also take over the Carrying Company. Then Lyon and
Lyon, who owned John Harker & Co. the tanker barge operators,
started contacting shareholders and during 1948 they bought all the
shares. In fact, they only wanted the tanker barges, and the dry cargo
barges, tugs and some motor boats were sold to the Docks and Inland
Waterways Executive of the British Transport Commission. The tankers
continued using the Severn Carrying Company name for some years,
but eventually the business was merged completely with Harkers.
Meanwhile, the traditional role of carrying dry cargoes to the Midlands
was continued by the DIWE, later to become the British Waterways
Board.

The new management concentrated on developing the barge traffic
between Avonmouth and Stourport. The principal vessels in the fleet
were the motor barges *Severn Trader*, *Severn Industry* and *Severn Merchant*, and the dumb barges *Severn Eagle*, *Severn Falcon*, *Severn Hawk* and
the six *Sabrinas*. When bringing a dumb barge from Avonmouth, the
crew were paid according to the load carried and so there was an
incentive to put in as much as possible until they were so low in the

water that it was said 'the sparrows could drink off the deck.' The old steam tugs *Severn Active* and *Severn Victor* were converted to diesels, as were most of the former Dock Company tugs that operated in the estuary and on the canal. A new motor barge *Severn Stream* was built by Charles Hill and Sons at Bristol in 1951, and this was followed by *Severn Side*, built by the Sharpness Shipyard Company in 1952. The DIWE also took over five of the Hill's motor boats with Petter engines, although these were soon transferred to the North West Division fleet. Two more were bought by Charlie Ballinger, who continued carrying for Cadbury's for several years.

Compared with pre-war days, the conditions of employment for the barge crews had changed considerably. The men had found that if they held out a bit, the firm would bend. They didn't actually strike, but if there was something they didn't like, they refused to go on board. The foreman couldn't sack them because he needed experienced men and it was no use bringing in total strangers. So it came about that everything was found for them. Each bargeman was supplied with a spring mattress and three blankets, and they were given a primus stove, oil lamps, crockery, cutlery and even some soap. If an old boatman had been provided with a pint of paraffin, he'd have thought it was his birthday! But even when the firm found everything for the youngsters, they still wouldn't sleep on board if they could help it.

In spite of strong competition from road and rail, good levels of general freight traffic were maintained during the 1950s, although it was almost wholly one way and very dependent on the arrival of ships at the Bristol Channel ports. Imports of grain and timber were carried from Avonmouth to Gloucester, and goods taken up the river included chemicals, sugar, cocoa, foodstuffs, steel, timber and lead. One outward cargo was home-grown grain, which was taken down to the mills at the channel ports. To help move large consignments quickly, four new dumb barges designated C/S 7 to 10 were built at Beaumaris and added to the fleet in 1959–60. At Worcester, a second transit shed was constructed on Diglis Wharf and, at Stourport, new piling was installed just below Redstone Wharf and a gantry crane was set up for unloading aluminium from barges.

Navigation of the river could still be difficult when there was a lot of fresh water, particularly at the Parting where boats had to turn into the main stream that flowed down to Maisemore Weir. On one occasion the motor tug *Progress* was towing a big heavy Bristol barge with *Severn Falcon* behind and as they met the main current, it nearly stopped them.

*Severn Merchant* and a *Sabrina* being loaded at Avonmouth

However, the second barge kept going on a slack rope and as it came out into the main stream, the current hit the bow and the rope snapped leaving the barge drifting towards the weir. The tug took the big barge into the bank, and the mate held them there with the engine going while the skipper walked back to see what had happened. The smaller barge only had a part-load of timber on for Worcester, and it had gone right over the weir. Contractors were building the new bridge at Maisemore at the time, and they had a wire stretched across the river to which they attached their crane barge. The drifting barge had broken this wire and ended up pushing some wooden frames together that were being used in constructing the new span. The tug couldn't go down because there wasn't enough water over the weir, so the skipper rang back to Gloucester to tell them what had happened. The foreman sent up a little motor boat that could go over the weir, but it wasn't powerful enough to tow against the current. Luckily enough, there was a big tide that morning, which pushed the barge back up over the weir with guidance from the launch, and then another tug took the barge on up to Worcester.

Petroleum traffic increased dramatically after the war. In the early 1950s, Harkers introduced several large motor barges capable of carrying up to 400 tons to Worcester, and later they also managed a number of

Harker's tanker *Westerndale* leaving Gloucester Lock on her way up the river. Note the check rope to prevent the bow being caught by the current

large tankers owned by Shell Mex and BP. Regent introduced more smaller barges for serving their depots at Gloucester and Stourport. Every morning, loaded tankers were waiting in the basin at Gloucester to go through the lock and up the river, and soon after they had all passed through, the tankers that had gone up the previous day came back empty. If when leaving Gloucester Lock there was any fresh water in the river, each tanker was supposed to have a check-line ashore, but some tried to do without. Then the current could swing the bow round, and quite a few ended up stuck across the channel going down to the weir. Once a tanker had gone across the stream like that, the water built up against the side, and it was very difficult to move. Even with two tugs, it wasn't always possible to pull the tanker clear, and often it had to wait until the next big tide.

There were numerous other instances of tankers getting into difficulties. As John Harker's tanker barge *Arkendale* was coming down the river empty one day, its engine broke down and so they carried on drifting down backwards with their anchor dragging along the bottom to give them some control. When they came to the Parting, they tried to get into the Gloucester water, but the main current took their stern end round and they started going down towards Maisemore weir. All they could do then was to loose more chain out and stop there on their anchor. Later a tug had to go and pull them up to the Parting and get them back to Gloucester. Another time, Harker's *Darleydale* was drifting backwards down the Gloucester channel, having lost her propeller, when her stern touched the bottom close to one bank, and the current swept her bow round so she became stuck right across the river. A second tanker tried to push her stern clear but became wedged between her and the bank, and a third tanker trying to help became sandwiched between the other two. All three were then stuck there blocking the river until the next high tide.

On their way up the river, one or two of the tankers ran aground near Hanley Castle and when the dredger was sent up there, they found a large amount of coal. There was a coal yard nearby, and while the boats were discharging over the years, a lot of coal must have gone into the river where the action of the water made the lumps rounded and polished into all sorts of forms. It is said that so much coal was pulled out by that dredger that it was enough to keep her boiler fired for a week!

One morning when the river was 18 ft above the sill of Gloucester Lock, a big tide brought the water right up to the canal level. Four

Regent barges were in the dock ready to come through, so the lock-keeper pushed all four gates open and let two of them out. He held the other two back in case the water level started to drop, but it stayed high and they went through as well. While this was going on, the lock-keeper had mixed feelings because he realized that if anything had gone wrong and the tide had started to drop, it would have emptied the canal. He was on edge until the last barge went out and he was able to close the gates. It was not something to try again!

By 1960, almost 500,000 tons of petroleum products were being carried each year to Gloucester, Worcester and Stourport, and the risks associated with this vital traffic were highlighted by a number of tragic accidents. In December 1958, John Harker's tanker *Darleydale* was coming down empty with a lot of fresh water in the river, and her wheel-house just hit one span of the Haw Bridge which crashed down killing her skipper. In October 1960, two other Harker tankers, *Arkendale* and *Wastdale*, collided in fog outside Sharpness. They were carried round the point by the tide, and they hit a pier of the Severn Railway Bridge, bringing down two spans. Both vessels caught fire and were a total loss, while five crew members lost their lives. In February 1961, *BP Explorer* overturned while on passage up to Sharpness, probably as a result of hitting a sandbank, and her crew of five were drowned. She was reconstructed as *BP Driver*, but in January 1962, she was caught in a rain squall and ran aground off Nash Point near Porthcawl. The crew of five managed to scramble ashore, but the vessel was a total loss.

During the 1960s, there were big changes in the traffic on the Severn. Shell Mex and BP outgrew their facilities at Monk Meadow Dock and established a new depot further down the canal at Quedgeley. Initially this was served by the existing tanker barges, but around 1970, these were largely replaced by new 1,000 ton coastal tankers introduced by Bowker and King. Also, the construction of oil pipelines removed the need for barges going up the river, so that Regent finished with this trade in 1969 and Harkers in 1975. General freight barge traffic also declined in the 1960s because the introduction of containers on deep sea shipping routes favoured ports near the Continent and as a result Avonmouth lost out. The freight traffic ceased altogether in the early 1970s, forcing the closure of the depots at Worcester and Stourport. Wheat shipments to the City Flour Mills in Gloucester came to an end as supplies were obtained by road. Reynolds Mill at Gloucester continued to receive wheat by boat, but this traffic also ceased when the business was closed down in 1977. After that, the only barge traffic was wheat

Regent tankers passing through Gloucester Lock with the river in flood. The
wheelhouses are folded down ready to squeeze under the Black Bridge

being carried to Healings Mill at Tewkesbury, but this gradually died out
as more and more of the wheat was brought in by road from local farms.
Also the closure of the oil depot at Quedgeley has virtually brought to an
end the regular visits of the coastal tankers. As all this traffic declined,
the vessels were sold and the crews had to find jobs ashore. The long
tradition of carrying goods on the River Severn and its connecting canals
has effectively come to an end – but the memories remain.

# APPENDIX

# *Tonnages Carried on the River Severn*

|  | 1915 | 1925 | 1935 | 1945* |
|---|---|---|---|---|
| Coal | 20,390 | 9,539 | 1,718 | 1,833 |
| Iron, iron ore, etc. | 5,252 | 2,714 | 10,717 | – |
| Metals | – | – | – | 22,692 |
| Stone | 13,145 | 428 | 50 | – |
| Salt | 16,569 | 4,148 | 215 | – |
| Bricks | 1,408 | 396 | 0 | – |
| Lime and sand | 8,349 | 4,642 | 2,346 | – |
| Pitch, tar and creosote | 20,159 | 13,384 | 9,697 | 4,341 |
| Petroleum products | – | – | 140,923 | 310,560 |
| Timber | 12,774 | 9,983 | 4,375 | 1,683 |
| Hay, straw and manure | 4,775 | 1,027 | 99 | – |
| Grain and flour | 72,439 | 67,521 | 50,567 | 67,931 |
| Foodstuffs | – | – | – | 15,427 |
| Sundries | 27,683 | 25,736 | 35,338 | 11,467 |
| Total | 202,943 | 139,518 | 256,045 | 435,934 |

* Scaled up from total for nine months.

Iron trow *Taff* loading from the Dominion Line steamer *Englishman* at Avonmouth 1910

# Glossary

| | |
|---|---|
| Beam | One of three strong pieces of timber across the hold to keep the sides in place. |
| Block rope | The part of the cut line passing through the pulley block on the mast and attached to a hook on the wing wall of a lock. |
| Cabin block | Wooden block on the cabin roof to support the stern plank. |
| Cloths or sheets | Waterproofed sheets of canvas used to protect the cargo. |
| Cratch | Triangular board at the fore-end of the hold and the frame supporting it. |
| Cut line | Cotton line used when a boat was towed by a horse on the cut. |
| Dunnage | Pieces of wood on which heavy cargo was laid to ease removal of the hoist chain. |
| False floor | Removable section of floor raised above the bottom of the boat so that a small amount of leakage or rain-water did not damage the cargo. |
| Farling | Strong rope to which the pig was attached and also sometimes used for towing. |
| Gate shutter | A short shaft used for closing a lock gate while standing on the opposite side of the lock. |
| Gunnel or gunwale | The rim around the top of a boat's side. |
| Gothams | Longboats based on the Stroudwater Canal. |
| Hatches | Cockpit behind the cabin of a horse boat. |
| Luby or looby | Pivoting metal pin on top of the mast to which the horse towing line was attached. |
| Mast | Wooden upright with iron top which could |

| | |
|---|---|
| | be adjusted in height within the mast box to get the horse towing line at the best level. |
| Pig | Iron bar weighing one hundredweight that could be dragged along the bottom of the river when drifting backwards under flood conditions. |
| Planks | Horizontal wooden planks running the length of the hold and supported by the mast-box, the two stands and the cabin block. |
| Severners | The deep-sided longboats with bluff bows used on the Severn. |
| Severn shaft | Long heavy shaft with two metal prongs on the end. |
| Shaft or hook-shaft | Wooden pole with a metal tip and hook (boat-hook). |
| Stand | Wooden upright slotting into a beam and used to support the planks. |
| Strap | Short length of strong rope used for checking the way of a boat as it entered a lock. |
| Stud | T-shaped piece of iron to which a rope could be attached. |
| Tippet | Narrow length of canvas to protect the cloths from being cut by the top strings and from being damaged by the boatman walking along the planks. |
| Timberheads | Wooden posts on either side of the foredeck to which the tug's towing rope was attached. |
| Top strings | Means of holding the top cloths in place over the planks. |

*River Severn and Canal Terms*

| | |
|---|---|
| Baccering | Allowing the horse to pull the boat unattended. |
| Bank full | The river level is up to the top of the banks due to a lot of fresh water. |
| Beam or balance beam | Horizontal extension of the top of a lock gate used for opening and closing the gate. |
| Bow-hauling | Pulling a boat with a rope while walking along the tow-path. |

| | |
|---|---|
| Bridge hole | The narrow section of canal under a bridge where the edge of the tow-path is lined with brick or stone, providing an easy place to step on or off a boat. |
| Butty | A boat without an engine that is towed by a motor boat. |
| Bye-trader | An individual or small firm operating one or a few boats. |
| Cutting | The approach to a river lock where there is no current as the main river is flowing over the adjacent weir. |
| Dead water | The static water in a lock cutting. |
| Dumb barge or dummy | A barge without a motor. |
| Fresh water | More water in the river than usual because of recent rain. |
| Hobblers | Men who helped work boats through locks or helped to unload boats etc. |
| Near side or inside | The side of the canal near to the tow-path. |
| Off side or outside | The side of the canal away from the tow-path. |
| Owner | Someone who owns his own boat. |
| Paddle | A board sliding in vertical grooves to control the water flow into or out of a lock, and also the winding mechanism above. |
| Peg the horse | Insert the peg on the end of the cut line into the loop on the horse's tackle. |
| Pound | Section of canal between locks. |
| Sill | Part of the bottom of a lock against which the gates fit. |
| Slack water | Where the flow is reduced in the shallow water near the river bank, particularly on the inside of a bend. |
| Stour Cut | The lower section of the Staffordshire and Worcestershire Canal where it follows the River Stour. |
| Tackle | The harness of a horse. |
| Thrum | Knotted silk cord tied on to the end of a whip thong to make the crack of the whip louder. |
| Windlass | Cranked handle used for raising lock paddles. |
| Worcester Cut | The Worcester and Birmingham Canal. |

# Sources

Anon., 'The Latest Canal Boat Development', *The Motor Boat*, 5 August 1932.

Anon., 'A New Type of Canal Carrier', *The Motor Boat*, 6 January 1933.

Anon., 'Six New Motor Canal Boats', *Motor Boat*, 4 January 1935.

Anon., *British Waterways – South Western Division*, Pyramid Press, *c.* 1965.

Conway-Jones, H., *Gloucester Docks – An Illustrated History*, Alan Sutton, 1984.

Farr, G., 'Severn Navigation and the Trow', *Mariners Mirror*, April 1946.

Faulkner, A.H., *Severn and Canal and Cadbury's*, Robert Wilson, 1981.

Faulkner, A.H., *Tankers Knottingley*, Robert Wilson, 1976.

Hadfield, C., *The Canals of the West Midlands*, David and Charles.

Richardson, L., *The River Severn between Upper Arley (Worcs.) and Gloucester*, Worcester, 1964.

Rowles, W., *Sharpness – The Country Dock*, Bailey Litho, 1980.

Stone, W.A., *A History of the Gloucester Harbour Trustees*, 1966.

Taylor, M., 'Severn Tanker Traffic', *Waterways World*, Nov/Dec, 1981.

Taylor, M., 'Longboats to Birmingham', *Waterways World*, November, 1983.

Wanklyn, M.D.G., 'The Severn Navigation in the Seventeenth Century: Long Distance Trade of Shrewsbury Boats', *Midland History*, Vol.13, 1988.

Cadbury Archives. Extracts from minute books and annual reports, 1929–48.

Gloucester City Library. *Gloucestershire Extracts*, Vol.4, pp.254–63; reminiscences of events in the early nineteenth century.

*Gloucester Journal*, 10 January 1791 and 30 November 1795, mishaps on the river; 23 January 1830, 20 February 1830 and 4 February 1832, steam tug; 12 May 1855, Severn Steam Tug Company; 5 October 1895, *Atalanta* to Worcester; 11 February 1939, tankers lost off Sharpness.

Gloucestershire Record Office D4764/4/16. Reminiscences of Severn boatmen collected by R.S. Stagg *c.* 1926.

Gloucestershire Record Office RI 31, CA 43 & CA 44. Severn and Canal Carrying Company publicity pamphlets.

Gloucestershire Record Office D2460, Box 53. Tonnages carried on the Severn.

National Waterways Museum, Cadbury's Collection. Reminiscences of Severn and Canal employees collected in 1947.

Public Record Office BT 31. Official records deposited at Companies House including an inventory dated 1891.

Public Record Office RAIL 829. Minute books of the Gloucester and Berkeley Canal Company.

Public Record Office RAIL 864. Minute books of the Sharpness New Docks and Gloucester and Birmingham Navigation Company.

Public Record Office RAIL 871. Minute books of the Staffordshire and Worcestershire

Canal Company.
Local directories.
Lloyds Registers of Shipping.
Mercantile Navy Lists.

# Index

183